T4-AKH-279

my shadowlife

by

Richard Bugajer

With a preface by Simon Wiesenthal

Edited by Reinhard Engel

Translated by Felix Plattner

Jewish Heritage

JEWISH HERITAGE
Published by The Jewish Heritage Project, Inc.
150 Franklin St., Suite 1W
NY, NY 10013, U.S.A.

Jewish Heritage is the publishing imprint of the Jewish Heritage Project, Inc. which gratefully acknowledges the generous support given to its International Initiative in the Literature of the Holocaust by: The Literature Program of the National Endowment for the Arts, the Literature Program of the New York State Council on the Arts, the New York City Department of Cultural Affairs, the Lowe II Foundation, and the Strochlitz Foundation.

First published in Austria as "Mein SchattenLeben: Eine Jugend im Ghetto und KZ," Czernin Verlag, Wien, 2000.

Copyright © Hava Bugajer, 2002.

All rights reserved.

Jewish Heritage gratefully acknowledges permission to use the art works and photographs from the Holocaust which enrich this volume, as granted by the following organizations, museums and archives:

YIVO, the Institute for Jewish Research, New York; The Jewish Historical Institute, Warsaw; Yad Vashem, Jerusalem; The Ghetto Fighters' House, Western Galilee, Israel.
Cover (fragment) painted in the Lodz Ghetto by M. Schwarz, 1942,
Used by permission of the Jewish Historical Institute, Warsaw.
Credits for artworks used are on p. 157, a continuation of this copyright page.

LIBRARY OF CONGRESS CATALOGUING IN PUBLICATION DATA
My shadowlife / by Richard Bugajer;
with introduction by Hava Eva Bugajer-Gleitman and preface by Simon Wiesenthal

1. Bugajer, Richard, 1928-1998. 2. Holocaust, Jewish (1939-1945)–Poland–Lodz–Personal narrative 3. Lodz, Auschwitz (Poland)–Ethnic relations. I. Bugajer, Richard II. Bugajer, Hava Eva III. Wiesenthal, Simon

DS135.P62L6441354   2002

ISBN, hardcover, 0-96604408-8; paperback, 0-9660440-9-6

Printed and bound in Canada by AGMV Marquis.
This book is printed on acid-free paper.
Book and cover design by James Taylor.

Without limiting the rights under copyright reserved above, no part of this publication may be reproduced, stored in or introduced into a retrieval system, or transmitted, in any form or by any means (electronic, mechanical, photocopying, recording or otherwise) without the prior written permission of the copyright owner and the above publisher of this book.

NATIONAL ENDOWMENT FOR THE ARTS

New York State Council on the Arts

956.94 BUG 2002

Bugajer, Richard 1928-1998
My shadowlife.

Table of Contents

Preface *by Simon Wiesenthal* .... *i*

Introduction: Reflections on Richard *by Hava-Eva Bugajer* .... *iii*

Prologue: Letter to Michael 1

1. September 1939: The Seance 5

2. An Idyllic Childhood
    – and Making a Mockery of the Jewish Students 9

3. School in the Ghetto 19

4. Apprentice in the Saddler's Workshop 25

5. Messenger Boy in the Tailor's Workshop 31

6. Falling for Fraud 37

7. Sarah 41

8. Hunger 45

9. My Summer as a Farmer 51

10. Curfew and Raid 55

11. Dreams of Freedom and Comrades 61

12. Apprenticed to the Electrician 63

13. Caught in the Mousetrap 69

14. Arrival at Auschwitz and My First Tallit 73

15. Drilled into Concentration Camp Inmates 79

16. The English Lesson 85

17. Marching Once Again 89

18. The Milk Soup 91

19. The Interesting Skull of an Ethnic Jew 95

20. The Reckless Optimist 101

21. The Death March 107

22. The Death of My Father 111

23. Ebensee 115

24. In the Tunnel 119

25. The Last Days 123

25. Rebirth 127

Epilogue 133

Editor's Note 141

Glossary and Notes 145

Biography of Richard Bugajer 149

Bibliography.. 151

Preface

by Simon Wiesenthal

Richard Bugajer's book has awakened painful and intense feelings in me. I hope that this important work will reach a wide American audience.

Hundreds of thousands of people -- mainly Jews or those who rejected or fought National Socialism -- lived a "shadow life" which in its deprivations, humiliations and dangers varied only slightly. These conditions varied according to the personality of the camp commanders, the momentary need for labor, or other circumstances to which these people, stripped of all rights, were exposed.

Immediately following the end of the Second World War, many survivors recorded their experiences during the Nazi period. They felt the responsibility as witnesses to report facts, to expose the true character of the criminal Nazi regime, and to prevent a repetition of the genocide.

But soon the political situation in Europe changed. The Soviet Union -- which with the Western Allies had won the War against the Nazis and *de facto* incorporated numerous East European states into its Communist sphere of influence -- became ambitious for the rest of Europe. The West had found a new enemy in Stalin. Soon the policies of the Western Allies toward Germany changed. The prosecution of the millions of crimes committed by Nazis suddenly lost priority. Internment camps for National Socialists were dissolved and convicted Nazi criminals were prematurely let out of jail and pardoned. The western part of Germany had become an ally against Stalin. This high tension between East and West lasted for approximately twelve years until the superpowers consolidated their spheres of influence and accepted one another. Looking back, it can be said that Stalin is to blame for the fact that youth today glorifies National Socialism and/or sees it as harmless.

Many survivors who attempted to lead a normal life and rebuild their families after the war wrote down their experiences to describe to the world what they had undergone in their own youth. As adults, they wanted to tell their children, so that they in turn would tell their descendants, and so on through the generations.

This political background was decisive in Richard Bugajer's promise to his son to tell his own story one day. His years after the war were filled with study and the development of his professional career. He began a family of his own. Only later did Bugajer bring his memories forward and wrote down the harrowing episodes of that time -- even though this process of remembering was a painful one.

Through this book, the reader will receive a personal account of the results of Nazi strategy to move the lamentable ghetto inhabitants from Lodz to do "voluntary work in the East." The inhabitants were initially "invited" -- "there is only room for 1,000 persons per transport" -- to sign up for this work. Everyone received two kilograms of bread and one kilogram of jam for the trip. Although many people were suspicious that this journey would not lead to work but to death, their hunger was stronger than their misgivings. Though Richard Bugajer's parents resisted the promises of the Nazis, ultimately they and Richard were transported out of the ghetto to the concentration camp.

The reader will also read how well-dressed, well-fed Jews from Germany, Austria, Belgium, and France arrived in the ghetto in regular train carriages with abundant luggage and leather suitcases and were surprised and appalled at the dreadful conditions in Lodz. In turn, they were observed suspiciously by the deprived, half-starved ghetto Jews who had been carted in open cattle cars from surrounding villages and towns. To make room for the newly arrived Jews, the Nazis had transported thousands of Jews earlier to Kulmhof (Chelmno), from where there was no return.

Richard Bugajer wrote down these experiences and kept revising and correcting them. Sadly, he died before he was able to complete the work.

I am convinced that today -- 55 years after the fall of the Third Reich -- his work has an important role. The number of witnesses to the Shoah is dwindling daily. This book and others of its kind will allow their children and grandchildren to better understand what their parents or grandparents suffered. It will also help the children and grandchildren of those responsible to be more aware of the terrible injustice done to the Jews, Sinti and Roma, Slavs, and other oppressed peoples by the National Socialists and their collaborators. In many European countries today, small groups of young people now band together as young National Socialists. May this book be an antidote of awareness to this phenomenon.

Simon Wiesenthal
Vienna, September 2000

Introduction: Reflections on Richard

by Hava-Eva Bugajer

"Now that I have almost completed my memoirs, I'm going on a cruise instead of finishing the job." These were Richard's words when we left home. "Time enough to finish it when we get back," was my answer. I proved to be a false prophet.

It was June, 1998, when we left home. We flew to Rome and embarked on the luxury liner on which we were to spend the following three weeks cruising the Mediterranean. It was the last of many beautiful vacations we had spent at sea.

We enjoyed Capri and Sicily. We spent a day on the island of Corfu. A barbecue on the ship's deck with music and dancing followed in the evening. That special night we danced and enjoyed it thoroughly. A couple of hours later that same night, Richard was dead. By that time, we were already back on the high seas. The ship turned around and brought us back to Corfu in the early morning. The beautiful island now looked ugly to me.

Richard and I had met in a Viennese café in October 1970. I had come to Vienna for a one-week visit before starting a six-month medical research job in Basel, Switzerland. Richard offered me a seat at his table and wanted to be my guide in Vienna. Since there were no vacant tables in the cafe, I accepted. At that time, he was beginning to organize his two clinics and was considering a third one. I was in the midst of my medical residency in Israel. Shortly after I decided to extend my stay in Vienna, an inquiry arrived from my mother asking what her daughter was doing in Vienna when she was supposed to be working on a research project in Switzerland. In January 1971, we were married in Israel. On our flight to Israel, we made a stop in Rome and stayed at the Hassler Hotel above the Spanish Steps. Many years later, we stayed in the same hotel before embarking on what would be our last cruise. So the circle closed.

When I met Richard, he was of middle height, obese, had thick grayish hair and very warm eyes under big glasses. The message he conveyed was: "Trust me, I will not disappoint you." When he walked, it was astonishing that despite his heavy build, he moved very fast and with an unusual lightness. The evening before I had met Richard, I had gone to the theater to see the musical "The Man of Lamancha." Richard thought it was symbolic; he, the man I met the next day, turned out to be my Don Quixote...

Now it is my duty to bring Richard's book to his readers – the fulfill-
ment of his last wish. He believed that reading and researching the
Holocaust was obligatory and should be performed for the sake of history out of an obligation to the dead and to spite the Nazi criminals. The
common reasoning "so that evil will not be repeated" was too simple for
his profound thinking. He held the opinion that the Shoah was a singular event that could not be repeated in the same form. He felt that com-
paring every evil with the Shoah and the transgressions of the Nazis is
wrong and diminishes the meaning of the Shoah. History never repeats
itself, because circumstances in the world are never the same. For the
Jewish people, the main difference today is the existence of the State of
Israel which empowers Jews all over the world.

Richard was not a man who liked to engage in small talk at cocktail
parties. He preferred deeper relationships and intimate dinners where
more profound matters could be discussed over exquisite food and wine.
He was a very good listener but, as our son has pointed out, he always
interspersed poignant remarks that showed his own depth of understanding. We had very interesting dinner parties in our home in Vienna
or in the homes of our friends, members of the Jewish and international community in Vienna.

Although he had the ability to develop a conversation with anyone,
Richard hated social hypocrisy and lies. Usually a mild and tolerant
man, he refused to make compromises in matters concerning Nazi criminals, the honor of the Jews, or the State of Israel. Very often, especially
in latter years, he expressed his opinions openly concerning Austria's
role in the Second World War and its aftermath. He brought attention
to the lack of punishment of Nazi war criminals and the growing ten-
dency to cover up conflicts rather than to conduct open discussions.

Richard always pointed out his wish that his memoir be read in the
United States and Israel. The original German version was only the first
step. He wanted Jewish children to be aware of their past so that they
would remain strong and proud of their people. He was a very proud
Jew and fond of his cultural heritage. I think he was very pleased that he
found in me a partner with some knowledge of Jewish history and culture. He wanted so much to transfer this heritage to our son. I spoke
Hebrew with our son and, during our life together, Richard tried very
hard to extend his own minimal knowledge of Hebrew from his two
years in the Itzhak Katznelson School.

Richard's relationship to Jewish culture was a secular one. Although
he believed in God, he was not observant. He had a conflicted relationship to the Jewish leadership during the Shoah, which at that time was

mostly religious, because of their misjudgment of the situation when Poland was invaded by Nazi Germany. Richard believed that the Jewish leadership should have advised the people not to obey the Germans right from the beginning, for example by resisting to wear the star of David. Though many might have been killed for this resistance, the Germans would have had a more difficult job and would have required more soldiers. Thus in the end, perhaps more Jews might have stayed alive. In his opinion, Jewish religious leadership failed completely, but never admitted their failure. This conflict – between his anger over the Jewish leadership which caused the Jews to accept their fate and his deep affiliation with the Jewish nation – was a part of his life, a part of his Holocaust past.

Richard began to write around the time of our first visit to Poland in 1989. He was invited to a conference dealing with the history of the Jews of Lodz. During that stay, he commissioned a professor of history in Lodz to research and write a paper on the history of his family, the history of the families Blawat, Dobranicki and Bugajer. The paper goes back to the beginning of the nineteenth century when his mother's ancestors took part in establishing the great textile industry in Lodz.

While Richard attended the conference, I went to Chelmno where Richard's grandmother was murdered. At that time, very little was done to commemorate the tens of thousands of Jews asphyxiated in the gas vans. We also went to Auschwitz-Birkenau where Richard had seen his mother for the last time. It was only natural that I was worried about Richard's health. Visiting this place – the symbol of the industrialized annihilation of European Jewry – might have a severe emotional and physical effect on any person, especially one suffering from cardiac disease. But it was very characteristic of Richard not to cry or complain about the past. He showed me the places where the trains had arrived, where his barracks had stood, giving me a detailed description of the facts. The word "suffer" was missing from all of his descriptions. Instead, he told me, "I feel good when I think about how I survived and lived to visit this place with you."

He only felt anger about the fact that no proper punishment of the Nazis had ever occurred. All his life, he raged that the perpetrators were never sufficiently punished. He liked Daniel Goldhagen's book *Hitler's Willing Executioners*, a condemnation of the perpetrators and their helpers, although he made a personal distinction between the criminals who committed the Nazi crimes and the "people" of Germany. In his opinion, the guilt of the perpetrators and the guilt of the entire German nation – or even of other nations which cooperated or ignored the guilt of the perpetrators – should not be combined and put on the same level. This would diminish the guilt of the murderers and help to excuse them. He always hated the murderers. He says in this book that he could never forgive the perpetrators, since the victims are dead – and no one has the right to forgive in their name.

In later years, he had fantasies of vengeance, of buying a gun and shooting Nazi criminals who had escaped legal punishment. Another idea was to privately publish a book containing the names of the criminals who had become respectable citizens, doctors, lawyers, judges. He had wanted to distribute their names within their current communities with the intention that their fellow citizens and neighbors would lose respect for them, but he was not sure that this would indeed be their reaction.

He felt bonded with Simon Wiesenthal, who devoted his life to bringing the Nazis to justice. He often quoted Wiesenthal with whom he shared his fury that the Nazis were not being punished. They spent time together talking about these matters. I was not a party to these conversations. They had a brotherhood between them – like people who bonded together as soldiers in a war or hostages or survivors of an earthquake.

Richard developed this feeling of brotherhood whenever he met with others who had survived the Shoah. Once at a dinner party, I saw Richard in deep conversation with a middle-aged man. There was nothing particularly interesting about him, but Richard later told me how much he had enjoyed their conversation. This gentile had been a prisoner in the Mauthausen Concentration Camp. When he was liberated, he worked for the American Army. His job was to catch Nazi criminals and arrange for their transportation. He treated them in the same way the Nazis had treated their prisoners. One day he threw his cap in the air, ordering a prisoner to bring it to him. As the prisoner went to retrieve his cap, he shot the prisoner. Later he told the American authorities that the prisoner had tried to escape. Richard told me, "At least that Nazi didn't escape the punishment he deserved."

Generally, Richard was a quiet, modest man, almost shy. This impression was sometimes misleading, because he could also be very strong and persistent concerning business, or when he thought that an injustice had been done to a person, especially to a Holocaust survivor. If someone aroused his pity, then all his toughness would vanish, and he might even act against his own best interests. Once in the streets of Vienna, a beggar approached us. Richard, who never passed a beggar without helping, gave him some money. Two streets further, the same man approached us and Richard gave him some more money. When I brought it to his attention that this was the same man and he looked like a drug addict, Richard responded, "Next time I won't give him anything." He thought there would be no next time but was mistaken. Several streets later, the same man approached – and Richard was still not able to refuse.

I recall another incident that occurred at a food shop. A man with a briefcase asked for the price of the "remains" of a sausage in a bun. The price was too much for him and he turned to go away. We assumed the man was hungry, but I didn't think he would accept help – he looked like an office worker, not like a beggar. Nevertheless, Richard talked to the man for a couple of minutes and returned to me. He asked me, "How do you think I made this respectable man accept money from me?" I had no idea. He had told the man, "Perhaps you are in some financial difficulties at the moment. Please take this money as a loan and when your situation improves you can pass it on to someone else who might be in need."

In the *Mishnah* there is a phrase: If you cast your bread on the waters, it will return to you in future years. I once mentioned this phrase to Richard and he adopted it as his motto. Money was just a tool for him. He liked to earn it and to spend it; it gave him freedom and independence. But he had no attachment to money. This was one of the lessons he learned from the Shoah. He liked to give better than to receive. The giving gave him far greater pleasure than the receiving. He derived no real happiness from receiving valuable gifts. For his birthday or our anniversary, he preferred to buy me a gift rather than getting one himself. He said that the Shoah had robbed him of the small pleasures in life. He was a very serious man. Only after many years together, seeing our son grow, did he achieve a certain amount of happiness.

Always fascinated by the financial world, he liked to gamble on Wall Street. Some professional financial advisers with whom I spoke after his death told me they had learned a lot from him. Richard was very disappointed that I didn't share his interest in business and that I influenced our son to ignore it completely. Only now – out of necessity after Richard's death – have I acquired some knowledge of financial management; I even find it interesting. Richard would have loved knowing this.

Richard enjoyed books, music, good food and traveling. In the last ten years of his life, he had a passion to travel and learn about new cultures. It was as if he felt it was his last chance. He had a wonderful bass voice and started to study music at the same time he studied chemistry and medicine. But because of his diminished lung capacity and lack of financial backing, it was more practical for him to stay with medicine. Still he enjoyed going to the opera and watching the techniques of the singers.

He had a childlike curiosity and was always open to new ideas and research in astrophysics and genetics. I remember our visit to the CERN Center, the experimental physics center in Geneva, where Richard was even more excited by what we saw than our son. Together we read about physics, genetics and other scientific research and later discussed these books.

Richard was different from many other survivors of the Shoah in that he never felt like a victim, but rather like a victor. Despite being alone after the war and suffering from tuberculosis, he was not broken and succeeded in graduating with his MD degree at the age of 25. He always spoke of the Shoah, but hated to be pitied as much as he rejected self-pity. He remained strong and powerful, even though his poor health forced him to abstain from physical activities. When he felt so ill that he couldn't accept an invitation, which happened often in later years, he preferred me to say that I did not feel well rather than to admit his own poor health. I suspect that the wrath he felt, although hidden, kept him strong and drove him on.

Richard asserted that after the Shoah, he had no homeland. Poland was merely the place where he was born and it didn't interest him. Austria was the place where he lived merely because that was where he was brought by the Nazis. He did however feel "at home" with the German-Austrian language and culture. He tried twice in his life to plan to settle in Israel: the first time as a student; the second time under my influence in the seventies. Both times it was his poor health – first his bad lungs, then his cardiac problems – that made him cancel his plans. He saw Israel as a homeland for the Jewish people, but felt it was too late for himself. He always supported Israel, seeing its establishment as a victory of the Jewish Nation over Hitler. Regarding his relationship to Israel, he often referred to Tom Segev's book *The Seventh Million* in which the author points out how the population of Israel – the seventh million – did not support the victims of the Holocaust. We both read the book and had many disputes about it, with me defending Israel.

Life with Richard was not easy. I was very independent and held to my own opinions. We fought almost every day. We had arguments about books and about how to bring up our son. Richard was over-protective and anxious when our son went skiing or horseback riding. We had different opinions about almost everything, but the disputes mostly ended with a laugh. Once our son asked, "Why do you and mama always fight?" Richard answered, "We just have different opinions."

After Richard died, I realized that I had come to accept many of his opinions that I had initially opposed. Although I hated management, today I manage his two clinics. I see this as my duty, since they were his achievements. One of these clinics was first established by a Jewish doctor in Vienna at the turn of the twentieth century. It was confiscated by the Nazis in 1938 and was returned to his son-in-law after World War Two. After his death, it was transferred to Richard by the daughter of the founder. I remember Richard saying to me, "I know you will manage things when it will become necessary."

Richard had a very close relationship with our son and wanted to pass on to him all his experiences of the past and his hopes for the future. He loved Michael as a baby, but waited impatiently for the time when he would be able to converse with him about profound matters. Richard had the ability to give much love and attention to me and to our son and needed our love and attention in return. Our family was very close. Richard was anxious about our son and about me, too. I thought that this related to the fact that he had been left alone in the world at the age of 17. Richard told our son never to consider a show of love as a sign of weakness, even though it may make you vulnerable. He told me that his parents' love for him had given him the strength to survive the Shoah.

The most remarkable thing I have done in my life has been to assume responsibility for the publication and distribution of Richard's memoir, this book, the product of his life. I am not sure that he believed that I would make such a major effort to get it published. When we first met, the Shoah was an abstract term to me, something that belonged to history; I was very forward-looking. For Richard, the Shoah was a part of his life, like a shadow that never left him. He always wanted me to understand this part of his life. If Richard is looking down from a cloud, he would be pleased to see that the Shoah has become part of my and our son's lives as well, as we try to bring his words to a larger audience.

I feel very grateful for knowing Richard. Living with him these wonderful years has been a gift. A friend recently told me that Richard was a man who felt no need to demonstrate dominance. Another friend asked me, "How could Richard have kept spoiling all of us, after what he went through?" His experiences in the Shoah helped form the overwhelming personality that his friends loved and trusted. His feeling of victory over the Shoah, his refusal to submit to the status of victim, and his tenacity in making his life a success made him a strong and generous man. These were the special features which caused his friends to love and admire him.

Reinhard Engel, who was one of Richard's admirers, has done the editorial work of pulling together the various texts that Richard left behind. He has done a wonderful job in creating this book and I am thankful to him for his careful handling of the written text.

Dr. Hava-Eva Bugajer, wife of the author
Vienna, January 2001

Dear Michael, my son,

To you, Michael, I promised to write the story down. I sat at your small bed and you asked me about your grandparents. I know – so many memoirs about the Shoah have been written already that my story could be considered repetitive. But everybody has lived through the Shoah both objectively and subjectively in his or her unique way and has responded differently. Thus I will tell you my story. You shall know what I experienced in my early youth. You shall read it to yourself and later read it to your children so that this horror does not fall into oblivion.

The people would be happy to forget all about it. Even today they are not ready to admit it; they do not want to be confronted with this disgrace. They are anxious and terrified of someone holding a mirror in front of their eyes and saying, "This is what you have done. You are capable of doing this – you, a mere intermediate stage of evolution that has not turned out very well, but is still pretending to be created in the image of the Creator."

Dear Michael, I hesitated for a long time, and since that evening at your bedside it has been two years. I could not bring myself to commit my memories and thoughts to paper. I was afraid of this recorded journey into the past, because in my thoughts and in my heart I face it every day since my rebirth – and it causes me pain. But probably this journey of return is the price I must pay for my rebirth.

The life I am living today is dynamic; it changes all the time: I am sick, then healthy again. I am successful, then failure strikes. I gain and lose weight. I dine at exquisite restaurants; I visit the opera and the casino. I earn a lot of money, then lose it again. I have good friends. I have a very good marriage with my wife. Sometimes I am annoyed with you, but I always love you, my son.

But my other life – the *shadowlife* – is ubiquitous. It stays static because I have already lived it; it cannot change anymore. It sticks with my present life, accompanies me everywhere all the time. Although it helps me to overcome obstacles, I have lost the ability to enjoy the small pleasures of daily life. The noise from my memories never ceases; in its rumblings lies the essence of my life. This is the price I must pay for living – for the balance in the accounts of my life – and the bill must be paid.

1

I write these first lines alone in a hotel room in Banff in western Canada, in the midst of the Rocky Mountains. You and your mother are on a trip to a glacier, up 2,600 meters. This is too high for me and too burdensome for my weak heart. I am surprised that writing comes so easily; I had imagined it to be far more difficult. I hope that I can complete my story, that it will be a book and that you, my son, will be able to read it.

You should not be afraid; do not fear, since the murderers have wounded your father but were unsuccessful in breaking him. I remained strong and am proud of it. I hope you too will be strong and that you will always keep in mind that my love for you is big enough to give you strength for your future life – even after I am gone.

Never lose your pride. Be proud of your people, your parents, your ancestors. You are a beautiful boy and you will be a good-looking man. Eager for knowledge and bright-witted, you are willing to learn and think clearly. These are valuable qualities in life that present responsibilities to you. Stay strong even when people out of envy try to oppress you. Should you experience failure, don't lose trust in yourself and in your abilities, but try to learn from it. Only if you remain strong will you be able to help others, to be supportive and a role model for them. Respect your fellow human beings and never consider love extended to you as weakness, for which it is too often mistaken. If you follow these rules, you will be happy in your life. Striving for happiness is placed in everyone's cradle. It is a natural aspiration for all human beings and the path and aim of our existence.

Richard and Michael Bugajer, 1997, in Lodz, Poland.

*Yitzhak Katznelson, well known poet,
educator and the author's teacher,
murdered in Auschwitz, 1944.*

September 1939
The Seance

One, two, three, four, five. The table moves five times. Above the table, we are holding hands – my mother, my father, my uncle Josef, the doctor, my grandmother and I. The room has been darkened. As the oldest, my grandmother gets to ask the first question: "How many weeks will the war go on?" The table moves five times: five weeks, no longer. The Germans cannot possibly fight much longer against Britain, France, Poland.

One, two, three, four, five.... I am eleven-and-a-half years old, a well-fed, chubby boy with jet black hair. If the war goes on for only five more weeks, I won't miss too much more of my school year. There is so much I want to learn.

I love my school. I am very happy that I managed to convince my father to send me there. Directed by Yitzhak Katznelson, it is a private school in Lodz. A Jewish private school. A rather expensive one. It was difficult for my parents to raise the money, even though they negotiated a cut in tuition.

I have already finished three levels of primary school there: the third, fourth and fifth grades. We are 44 boys, all friends. There is no envy among us, no hate, no differences – as there used to be between Poles and Jews in the public school I previously attended.

I still remember my first day at Katznelson's school. I was wearing the mandatory public school uniform: short navy blue trousers, knee-high socks, and a blue formal jacket with red epaulettes. My new classmates were looking at me in astonishment and admiration. They were all wearing plain clothes and suddenly in walked a boy in uniform! They didn't know this was the only suit I owned.

In this school, the teachers like us and care for us. Yitzhak Katznelson teaches Hebrew. His brother Moshe teaches Bible and religion. Other subjects include Polish, history, arithmetic, geography, drawing, handiwork, physical education and singing. I am always one of the best students in class. Only Hebrew and Bible are difficult. These subjects were new for me and we couldn't afford private lessons for me to catch up. Nevertheless, at the end of last year, I received an award for being one of the best pupils.

Occasionally, there are performances at school, and I sometimes sing in an auditorium filled with students and parents. Most of the songs are original compositions by Yitzhak Katznelson. At the end of the performances, we always sang *Techesakna*, the song of the Zionist movement, and *Hatikva*, the Jewish anthem.

I hope the oracle was right about the five weeks! I want to see my friends in school and sing *Techesakna* and *Hatikva* as soon as possible.

Richard Bugajer (standing on the left)
in his family circle in the 1930's.
Standing (third from right) is Richard's father;
reclining (second from right) is Richard's mother.

An Idyllic Childhood – and Making a Mockery of the Jewish Students

I was not born in Lodz, but rather in Kielce, in 1928. This was where my parents and my father's three brothers lived with their families. My father traded in wood and, with his brothers, ran a sawmill where the wood was processed. The Depression of the 1930s hit him hard. He had bought forest lots in the eastern part of Poland and lost his money when wood prices collapsed. My father was an honest and decent man. He paid for everything he bought and did not want to be in debt. So after the collapse of his business, we were left with very little.

In Kielce, we had a nice flat on Koscinski Avenue. I played in the backyard with my friends who lived in our building or nearby. At that time, I attended Cwiczeniowska, a very good public school which was considered elite. But I did not like it, because it was there that I first encountered anti-Semitism.

There were four Jewish children in class, all sitting in the last two rows. When the Catholic priest came to teach religious lessons, the four of us had to leave the room, amidst derisive laughter from the other children. Religious study was mandatory at school and we had a teacher of our own.

I was a good student and our teacher, Mr. Rubik, was impartial in the grades he gave me. Though he never discriminated against me, he didn't like me very much. The atmosphere in our school was very bad. During recess, there were often ugly fights between us four Jewish students and the others.

Back home we were a big family. My father had six brothers, five sisters, and some nieces and nephews. My father's parents lived in Sedziszow. While I can not remember my grandmother at all, I vaguely remember my grandfather. I believe he traded in wood as well. Sometimes I spent summers there with my parents. There we met other members of the family: uncles, aunts and cousins.

According to what friends of my grandparents later told me, their house was always open. Not only family members, but also neighbors and friends passing through were always welcome – even overnight. My grandfather wore traditional Jewish clothing, so one can assume he was observant and closely bound to Jewish tradition. My father, on the other hand, was an agnostic. I can not remember ever having seen him go to the synagogue. But he always felt he belonged to the Jewish people.

My parents were both high school graduates. My father, who was born in 1895, obtained his degree in from Russia. After *Gymnasium*, my mother attended university in Cracow, but I don't know whether she finished her studies. At that time, it was unusual for a female to attend university. My mother played the piano beautifully. She also had a very good singing voice which I inherited. When I was a child, she sat at my bedside in the evenings and read fairytales to me.

At home, our everyday language was Polish, This was the language in which I wrote, read and dreamt. I shared all my thoughts with my father, often talking for hours. Even later, in my adolescence, I discussed everything with him. We discussed politics, books, even my sexual problems while I was going through puberty. I didn't keep any secrets from him; we were the closest of friends.

With one exception, I was never punished, let alone beaten, by my parents – though I am sure I might have deserved it, now and then. My lively imagination made me think of the nastiest tricks. Once, a friend and I dressed up as beggars and went begging in the streets. When I came home and my father found out, he was very angry with me. That was the only time he slapped my face.

My imagination was quite well developed. One day, I told my parents about a theatrical performance at school in which I was going to play the leading role. I described my part in the most minute detail. Every day, my parents asked about my progress and about the day of the performance – until one day my parents found out that it was pure imagination on my part.

In Kielce, we lived in a very nice flat with unusual dark wooden furniture. There were three large rooms, one smaller one and a kitchen with a stove fired by wood or coal. Displayed on top of the cupboard was a photograph of me as a naked baby. This disturbed me immensely! Every time we had guests, I was embarrassed when they saw me in "this state." I was tempted to tear it up or to let it "disappear," but I could not find the courage to do it.

In the evenings, my parents frequently went out to a club where they played cards or listened to music. Meanwhile, I stayed home with the nanny. She was young, perhaps thirteen or fourteen. Once, she shared my bed with me and I was determined to find out if she had a penis like me. So, at the age of five, I experienced my first sexual feelings. Although the nanny was with me, I was always frightened when my parents left. Sometimes I vomited with fear. Perhaps it was just my way of protesting.

Our holidays were spent either at my grandparents' house or in the villages of Slowik and Zalesie near Kielce. In the country, I played with other children, especially with my cousins. The journey into the holidays was always exciting. We took a train and at the railway station we rented a coach drawn by horses. I was allowed to sit on the box beside the coachman. From up high, I could watch the horses and the view of the town as we rode by. But what impressed me most was one day when a horse raised his tail to relieve himself; the big balls were fascinating to me.

There is something else I remember from my early childhood. One day as I was walking down the main street leading to the railway station, I saw my father coming out of a cafe on the other side of the road. As I ran towards him, I was run over by a policeman on a bicycle. Fortunately, I was not hurt. I was frightened, that was all.

Despite our financial troubles, I must say I had a very happy childhood in Kielce.

My father saw no opportunities for building up a business again in Kielce. Therefore in 1935, we moved to my mother's parents' home on Strzelcow-Kaniowskich Street in Lodz. It was a two-family house belonging to my grandfather. My grandparents lived on the upper floor. My grandmother was a stately, well-educated woman. She was the daughter of a wealthy businessman who had sent her to the best schools. She spoke fluent German, her mother tongue, and Polish. She read the German classics. My grandfather died in 1939, before the war began.

My grandparents' house had a little garden where I played with other children. One of the girls was Haneczka Gliksman and we were very close. We played the usual games, such as "house" and "doctor."

Later, my grandfather sold the house and we moved into a four-room flat on Legionow Street. There were five of us: my grandparents, my parents and I. My mother's brother Josef, who had studied medicine in Paris, returned to practise in Poland. He earned his living by making house calls to patients on the recommendations of older, better established colleagues, as well as giving injections. Because he did not have much work, I spent a lot of time with him, playing and talking.

11

The flat on Legionow Street had a small square anteroom without windows, but with a glass door which allowed the light to enter leading to my grandparents' library. There, my father, my uncle and their friends played bridge in the evenings and on weekends. I was often allowed to stay and joke with them. Their game fascinated me and I learned to play bridge by watching.

I borrowed books from my grandparents' library at random and read authors such as Alexandre Dumas, Karl May, Henryk Sienkiewicz, Romain Rolland, Victor Hugo, Juliusz Slowacki, Leo Tolstoy, Julian Tuwim and Nikolai Gogol. When I finished a book, I talked with my father about it and he explained whatever I had not understood. As I lay in bed in the evenings, I cut out pictures of knights from my grandfather's leather-bound books, imagining battles from the Polish Uprisings of 1830 and 1863. My youthful imagination had no boundaries.

When we moved to Lodz, I told my father that I never wanted to attend a Polish public school again. In Kielce's primary school, I had painfully experienced being a Jew. But I didn't let this depress me. I was born a Jew, I remained a Jew and I proudly viewed myself as a Jew – without arrogance, but also without inferiority. Just as a German is a German, an Englishman is an Englishman, an Austrian is an Austrian, or a Pole is a Pole.

The following years – the third, fourth and fifth grades of the Jewish primary school – were a happy time for me. My fellow students and I stayed together as friends. Our teachers not only cared for our education, they also loved us.

Some of my friends from school were later in the ghetto with me. Out of 44 students, six survived the war. This is a "high ratio" – more then ten percent – considering that only three percent of all Polish Jews survived. Today, Henek Waks lives in Toronto, Zehim Ehrlich in Israel, Kuba Widawski in Melbourne. Wollmann immigrated to the United States before the war and now lives in New York. Rappaport was not in the ghetto; he survived the war with fake Aryan papers. I don't know where he lives today.

The life that became my "shadowlife" began early in September 1939. At the time, I was a little older than eleven, thirsty for knowledge, a model student, a spoiled only child. By then, our economic situation had improved again. My mother had a fur coat and I was given a fur collar for my coat.

Now and then, I was allowed to go to the cinema by myself. My father gave me fifty *groschen*, the price back then for one of the poorer seats. I saw cowboy films featuring Tom Mix or Laurel and Hardy.

12

The last film I saw with my parents was *Madame Walevska*, featuring Charles Boyer and Greta Garbo. Before the screening, my father bought a bar of dark chocolate that we – or, to be honest, for the most part I – finished during the movie. Since I was a plump child, eggs were crossed off my breakfast menu; chocolate milk was also off limits – too fattening.

In 1939, I spent the last of my school holidays with my cousin Roman Tuchschneider at his parents' villa in the countryside of Romanowka. Our life was still carefree at that time. We quarrelled about who was going to read Karl May's *Winneto* first. We went swimming and rowing in the lake and thoroughly enjoyed our school holidays. My mother travelled with me and my father came to visit us every weekend. After the holidays, my sixth grade of primary school was about to begin.

At the end of the long vacation, I noticed tension amongst the grown-ups, without knowing the specifics. They talked about war. England and France had entered into an alliance with Poland, Russia with Germany. The Germans had delivered an ultimatum to Poland concerning Danzig and its corridor. My father was very nervous. On one hand, he was afraid of the Nazis; on the other hand, he hated the Bolsheviks. Escape to Russia was therefore out of question. Something strange and frightening was in the air.

On September 1, 1939, war broke out, and my life changed abruptly and fundamentally. We fled from Lodz on that very day. The Germans immediately bombed Lodz and all the access roads, including those leading to Warsaw – but we were determined to flee there. I, my mother, my uncle, my father, and my grandmother. It seemed the entire city of Lodz was on the move. All roads were blocked by endless lines of horse carts and carriages. Since we couldn't move forward by carriage, we walked carrying our backpacks.

We didn't get very far. After five, ten or fifteen kilometers, we decided that I was to return with my mother and grandmother. My father and uncle continued on to Warsaw to defend the capital.

When we returned to Lodz, life was not easy We had very little money. My mother could only afford some sacks of potatoes and coals for cooking. Soon she found a job in the employment office of the local Jewish community and earned a little money.

After Warsaw surrendered, my father came back to Lodz, while my uncle remained in the capital.

I don't know whether my father fought in Warsaw; I never asked him. I don't think he did, since he never mentioned it.

The confiscation of Jewish property began as soon as the city was occupied. First Jewish businesses were seized. Later Jews had to surrender their jewellery, fur coats, and other valuables – even their stamp collections. Jews were even forbidden to keep pets. Their dogs, those faithful companions, were shot.

At the end of February 1940, we were forced to move to the ghetto. It was already dangerous to be in the city; every day people disappeared. The German authorities gave orders that all Jews had to move to a certain area of town, the slums.

So we moved. We loaded our personal belongings onto a wooden cart with those few pieces of furniture we hoped to fit into our new quarters. Approaching us from the other direction were the Poles who were being resettled from the slums.

Compared to the nice apartment where I now live in Vienna, the four rooms at my grandmother's house were a modest lodging. But by comparison, the single room in the ghetto on Brzezinska Street really was a hovel.

A hundred years ago, my ancestors built the part of town where the Lodz Ghetto stood. They never imagined that they were building the anteroom to the death chambers of their families and their people.

In 1939, Lodz had 700,000 residents, among them 233,000 Jews. The German troops occupied us on September 8, 1939. Immediately thereafter, the reprisals and riots against the Jews began. Jewish property was confiscated. Bans were placed on the use of public transportation. Jews became the victims of curfews, assaults, forced labour and displacements. In December 1939, the yellow star – which Jews were forced to wear on their front and back – was introduced.

First the occupying forces drove thousands of Jews out of Lodz into the so-called Generalgouvernement. *Then, early in February 1940, the ghetto was established. At the end of April 1940, the ghetto was hermetically sealed off. Thus the ghetto of Lodz, called "Litzmannstadt" in German, was the first to be cut off from the outside world.*

There were 140,000 people imprisoned in the Lodz Ghetto. No smuggling nor contact with the Polish resistance was possible. Whoever came too close to the barbed wire fence bordering the ghetto was shot by the police who guarded the ghetto. Hans Biebow, a coffee merchant from Bremen turned Nazi administrator, was assigned head of the ghetto administration. The daily rate for food supply was set to 30 pfennig per person; later it was reduced to 19 pfennig. First the Kripo, the criminal police, and the Gestapo terrorized the Jewish population and made them surrender all their valuables. Later the ghetto administration succeeded in having these funds credited to the administration, so they could buy food for the inhabitants.

The Jewish leader of the ghetto, Mordecai Chaim Rumkowski, called the "eldest," set up a city within the city in the Lodz Ghetto. There was a registration office, a housing office, a health department and several hospitals, a bank with the ghetto's own money, kindergartens, an old people's home, a prison, groceries and a Jewish police force. There was even a cultural center where symphonies were occasionally performed.

The economic base consisted of workshops, so-called Ressorts, working mainly for the German Wehrmacht, but also for private companies, for example the Neckermann Department Store. Rumkowski's motto was: "Work is your passport to survival. Law and order must rule in the ghetto."

In the autumn of 1941, another 20,000 Jews from Berlin, Vienna, Prague, Frankfurt, Hamburg, Düsseldorf and Luxemburg arrived. Also 5,000 Roma from the Austrian province of Burgenland were interned on the edge of the ghetto.

In December 1941, Rumkowski received orders to gather 20,000 Jews for work outside the ghetto; he managed to reduce that number to 10,000. At the end of January 1942, these 10,000 people – misled into believing that they were being taken for a working mission in the countryside – were murdered at the nearby Chelmo camp. A month later, there was a second series of deportations lasting until early April 1942. This time 34,000 people were deported and murdered. In the next two months, another 10,000 Jews from Germany, who had arrived at the ghetto the previous November, were taken to Chelmo and murdered. By the end of 1941, the 5,000 Roma from Burgenland had also been sent to the gas chambers in Chelmo and were asphyxiated there.

From the "Warthegau" – the Polish territory near the German border that had been annexed – 14,000 people were taken to the ghetto. In this way, the towns and villages surrounding Lodz, mostly inhabited by Jews before the war, were depopulated.

In September 1942, the ghetto was blocked off hermetically. Then German terror units emerged in the ghetto. Sixty people were shot on the spot; little children, babies, old and sick people were thrown from windows onto trucks. Everyone below the age of ten and above sixty was taken to Chelmo and murdered. In addition, 40,000 people died of hunger and disease by 1944.

In June 1944, those listening to the radio illegally were arrested and executed. Between the second half of June and the middle of July, another 7,000 residents of the ghetto were taken to Chelmo and murdered. But, when the Red Army stood at the Vistula River, the rate of killings was not fast enough for the Germans. Another extermination camp was

15

used for the residents of the ghetto: Auschwitz-Birkenau. Sixty-five thousand people were taken there. About 45,000 were sent to the gas chambers immediately upon arrival; 20,000 were destined for death through labor.

In the Lodz ghetto, only 600 Jews were left to clean up. Another 270 managed to hide. On January 19, 1945, the Red Army rescued them.

*One thousand eight hundred students
attended the Marysin School.*

School in the Ghetto

True love to the grave,
I swear to you with heart and hand.
Whatever I am and whatever I have,
Praise to you, the Fatherland.

I learned this poem from a German textbook 58 years ago at school in the ghetto. I still remember it. I don't know why. I keep forgetting things I read only a week or a day ago. I think it's progressing senility; I'm getting old. But the fact that I have lived to this age is a miracle, mere chance – perhaps destiny.

At school in the ghetto, we are taught four languages: Polish, German, Hebrew and Yiddish. I'm glad the school was opened in April 1940. Rumkowski, the Jewish director of the ghetto, delivers an address. We are urged to be good students, to learn diligently, and he will take care of us. Then he hands out candy to the children.

The school is in Marysin, a very long distance from our new flat. I go there early each morning and don't return until three in the afternoon. Eighteen hundred students attend the school. In my class, I see old friends from Katznelson's school. There are also older boys from the Hebrew High School, as well as boys and girls from other schools.

In the beginning, we must study very hard, since we have already missed six months of school, and the teacher wants us to catch up. But I am so glad to be among children of my own age again. Besides, we get soup at lunch time. And that is important for me, since I am hungry all the time.

The food rations are meager. Mama works at the housing office in the local community. My father does construction work outside of the ghetto; I think he is a foreman there. He is experienced with wood and construction materials. Since both my parents are working, we get along

19

quite well by ghetto standards. There are so many people without work who are far worse off.

Before the war, my father came home from work at about six o'clock. I waited for him and joined him for dinner. Then I told him what had happened in school during the day. Sometimes, I repeated some swear words that I had picked up at school or on the street and waited anxiously for his reaction. Sometimes, I asked him if I could borrow some erotic books from his library, or for 50 *groschen* to see a cowboy film at the local cinema. Now and then, I sampled his food. This half hour in the evening together was very important to me.

Now, in the ghetto, my father must get up at five. His squad leaves at six for work. He takes his lunch with him. Mama makes a thick potato soup the evening before.

In 1986, I took part in a medical conference in New York. I lived at the Hotel Pierre, one of the finest in New York, and had planned to visit my friend the historian Lucjan Dobroszycki and the writer Isaac Bashevis Singer. But Lucjan was on the West Coast at the time and Isaac was in Florida. So I went to the YIVO Institute of Jewish Research and visited the archives to amuse myself by looking for documents from the Lodz Ghetto.

While flipping through the index, I noticed the title of a document containing the statement of a certain Mrs. Bugajerow, close to my name but spelled differently – in itself, that didn't strike me as significant. I asked for duplicates of some ghetto decrees, bulletins about rations, as well as the statement by "Mrs. Bugajerow."

When I held that piece of paper in my hand, it seemed to me like a voice from another world. The document contained a 1940 testimony given by my mother in the Polish language, apparently to a representative of an American-Jewish organization – maybe the Joint or YIVO. I felt as though I had been struck by lightning; I became terribly excited. Yet it was by sheer coincidence that I had come across this valuable memento in New York – all because I had been bored and did not have anything better to do.

In this statement, my mother took care to express with caution her view of the forced labour of Jews following the German occupation of Lodz. She stated, "The employment office was installed to make Jewish labour available to the Germans. As compensation, the community received 1.75 mark per day for men, 1.25 mark for women and 2.25 mark for skilled workers. But this payment only applied to persons who volunteered for work. Those who were picked up on the streets and forced to work received nothing.

"The relationship between the authorities and the workers was good. Sometimes the Germans even intervened on the side of their workers to the community, so they would receive their daily payments. But the slightest lapse was severely punished. When a Jewish worker who had been toiling some weeks for the Totenkopf-Standarte, a special SS unit, was accused of stealing a piece of coal found in his coat, he was shot. For the smallest mistake, workers were beaten and tortured. Four ethnic Germans were assigned as supervisors for each employment office.

"The daily total paid out by the Jewish community amounted to between 2,000 and 3,000 mark. Very often the community could not come up with this money. The Gestapo employed about 1,000 workers, the Totenkopf-Standarte 200 to 300, and there were forced laborers working for other Nazi organizations. To raise the money needed for the workers, the community collected taxes from those who did not work. Later, cars picked up Jews to work outside the ghetto. The Germans didn't pay for this work, but forced the community to pay the workers. Working for the Gestapo was dangerous; Jews tried to avoid this work although the pay was twice as high."

I'm hungry. I'm hungry all the time. Often I cannot restrain myself. I reach into my father's plate and grab some potatoes. Then I have terrible twinges of remorse. My father is starving too and must work hard. Nevertheless, I have stolen from him, my beloved father. I think he notices sometimes, but he never says a word.

The ghetto is a self-contained unit, hermetically sealed, fenced off with barbed wire. Armed and uniformed guards patrol everywhere. At the entrance of the ghetto, there is a big sign which reads: "Attention! Jewish area! Keep out! Danger of epidemics!" The guards, recruited from the 101 Police Battalion, enjoy shooting indiscriminately at people who walk near the fence or live nearby. Almost every day, several people fall victim to this kind of "fun."

Hunger and disease, mainly tuberculosis, take a growing toll. People collapse in their hovels, on the streets or at work. Frequently, they vomit blood and die shortly thereafter. Because their relatives don't have money for a burial, the corpses lie in the streets until they are eventually loaded onto a cart by a funeral squad. They are taken to a big pit and buried there.

Often, I walk right by the dead bodies. Over time, the sight doesn't impress me anymore. For me, life goes on. I have the firm intention to survive and push aside any thoughts of my own death. *Apparently, it's hard to imagine one's own death.*

At school, as well as at home on afternoons, I study diligently, since I need to make up for lost time. Under no circumstances do I want to lose a year. I have passed the sixth grade exams and am doing well in the first year of secondary school. I believe that when the war is over – which will be soon I hope – I will graduate at the age of eighteen.

After homework, I read a lot; I literally devour books. For one *mark* a month, I can borrow books at the public library. I read everything that I come across: Polish, French and Russian writers. They help me build a world of dreams.

In July 1941, I finish my first year of secondary school. We are supposed to start again in September, but meanwhile transports carrying Jews from the neighbouring towns arrive in the ghetto. Space must be made to accommodate them. Our school is assigned to house them. Hitler has attacked Russia and has given orders to murder all European Jews. At the time, of course, I am not aware of this order. I live in my world of dreams.

Sometimes in the distance, I hear the muffled footsteps of soldiers who march eastwards. They are singing songs such as "*Denn wir fahren, wir fahren, gen Engelland, gen Engelland...*" (As we march towards England...) or "*Wir werden weiter marschieren, wenn alles in Scherben fällt...*" (We will keep marching even if the world goes down) or "*Heute gehört uns Deutschland, morgen die ganze Welt...*" (Today Germany is ours, tomorrow the whole world). I like these melodies. I am not yet able to comprehend the deadly danger suggested by their lyrics.

L.W. Nixon Library
Butler County Community College
901 South Haverhill Road
El Dorado Kansas 67042-3280

Shoemaker's workshop in the Lodz Ghetto.

Apprentice in the Saddler's Workshop

In the autumn of 1941, it is becoming apparent to me and my parents that the school in the ghetto will not be opened again. New transports are arriving from the surrounding town and all these people need accommodations. The ghetto is bursting at the seams.

My parents engage a tutor for me so I won't miss too much schooling. They find a very well-educated, unmarried man of about thirty, skinny as most are in the ghetto – and without work. He is pleased to be able to earn a few marks per month. The lessons take place in our dwelling on Brzezinska Street. When the weather is nice, we study in the yard behind the house. Twice a week, the teacher comes for two hours and teaches me algebra, German, Hebrew and the Bible. He gives me homework to complete before the next lesson, at which time he checks to make sure I have understood everything and whether I have been diligent. I like my tutor very much.

At the end of 1941, our economic situation becomes more difficult. We must dismiss my tutor. My father can no longer work outside the ghetto; it has become too dangerous. Miraculously, he finds a new job in a food refectory, right on our street. Nevertheless, my parents decide that I should look for a job in a workshop to earn some extra money. Coincidentally, a list of former pupils from the ghetto school has been sent to a saddler's workshop and they give me a job.

I am probably the worst worker at the saddlery. Sitting on a saddler's chair, I sew coat belts. The space between seams should be exactly ten millimeters, but I just can't manage to get it right. Other boys my age manage to finish six or even seven coat belts a day. I finish three at the most, and two of those are worthless. Since we are paid by the piece, I get very little money at the end of the month. As punishment, I sometimes don't receive the daily soup, so I'm hungry all day long.

About fifteen years ago, I saw a performance of Bertolt Brecht's "Three Penny Opera" at the Vienna Burgtheater. The scene at the end

25

of the play, when Mack the Knife is hanged, reminded me of the following incident from the ghetto.

One day, all workers in the saddlery are taken to a square where an execution is about to take place. Slowly the square fills with people, as employees from other factories and workshops join us.

In the middle of the square, the gallows have already been raised. The convicts are standing in a row behind the gallows, waiting to be hanged. I don't know why they will be hanged; no one knows the details. Some say that they have been charged with having spread rumors and upsetting ghetto residents. Others say they have stolen leather, property of the Third Reich.

Among the convicts, there is a boy, who is perhaps twelve years old, younger than I. We must wait. Gestapo soldiers are here, and the Jewish police stand at attention as well. The victims don't cry or beg for their lives. Quietly, they step on the wooden footstools. Each of them has a rope around his neck. Then the footstools are kicked away from under them.

They hang in the square for 24 hours. Some have their tongues hanging out – a terrifying sight. We march past the hanged men and then go back to work.

But life goes on and eleven dead men do not make a difference. To me this is of little importance; I have already seen so many corpses on the street, starving people, those dying of diseases, old people and children. In most cases, only the skeletons are left, and they are loaded on a cart and brought to the cemetery.

Now and then, on my way to work, I see someone and immediately recognize he is doomed. He has hollow cheeks, his eyes look strange and he moves like a zombie. I think to myself, he will not live for another two weeks. But apart from that, I don't pay much attention to the dead.

I am hungry all the time and at night I dream of food.

Our supper consists mostly of hot salted water with a few turnips swimming on the surface. Sometimes when there is a ration of potatoes, a few thin potato slices are added. The sparse oil assigned to us is not used for soup. No drop of that precious fluid is wasted. Each of us puts his slice of bread into it; bread tastes wonderful with the dark oil.

We get our bread from a food allocation office. Officially, it should weigh two kilograms, but very often it is only 1.95 or even 1.90. The remainder has no doubt been stolen by the bakers. We are glad when the bread is old, because it is easier to cut. And 250 grams of old bread are more than 250 grams of fresh bread; at least, that is how it seems to me. The food rations in the ghetto are not consistent. There are weeks without any potatoes; other times there are five kilograms for each person.

Often the vegetables are spoiled and the rations meager. Other times, we receive several cartloads of varied vegetables. For ten days, the portions are split according to the stock levels: sometimes 100 grams of sugar, other times 250. Now and then 250 grams of rye flakes, sometimes only 50. There is also coffee substitute from the Meinl Company. It tastes terrible.

Meanwhile, I am hungry all the time. My thoughts focus on trivial things such as potatoes. I dream of eating my fill, of having enough potatoes for a change. A big bowl filled with hot potatoes – that is my deepest desire. Having enough bread, whole loaves of it – this seems so desirable and unattainable to me that even thinking of it seems like a sin.

On the black market, food prices vary. On average, a loaf of bread costs between 600 and 2,000 *marks* of ghetto money. My mother makes 55 *marks* a month, my father 80, and I hand over 30 out of my 35 *marks* to my parents. With that, we can just about pay for our meager food rations. Buying on the black market is out of the question.

Sometimes there is a ration of canned horse-meat, one can for three people. Usually we sell the meat to raise money; our clothes and shoes look very tattered.

With the money we earn, we are just able to buy what is absolutely necessary – that means whatever is available for food stamps. I keep five *marks* of my apprentice pay to buy old textbooks. Of course, not all books are available, but I can still continue to study physics, history, Latin and German.

Three or four years ago, I visited the Vienna synagogue for the Yom Kippur service. On that occasion, the Austrian Federal Chancellor Dr. Franz Vranitzky and Vienna's Deputy Major Hans Mayr came to the synagogue. These two gentlemen certainly were not anti-Semitic, and their presence was meant as a gesture of respect and sympathy for the Jewish community. The Viennese Jews were pleased about the visit and considered it a great honor. But this respectfulness towards the politicians was shown in an excessively servile way by some members of the Jewish community. That visit and the behavior of some of the Jews aroused unpleasant feelings in me and stirred up memories of another visit, back in the Lodz Ghetto.

During my time in the ghetto, I went to the synagogue on Franciszkanska Street on Yom Kippur. I had not been brought up religiously, but out of curiosity I wanted to see the synagogue and what people were doing there. Suddenly all the people in the synagogue stood up as uniformed SS men, Gestapo officers and civilians from the ghetto administration entered. Several Jewish officials eagerly hurried to make room in the front rows for the high ranking visitors. The officials took the seats emptied for them and watched the service for two hours without interrupting, then left again.

I don't know why I feel the need to draw parallels between these two visits. It seems that the submission of some of my fellow believers in Vienna disturbed me when they welcomed their guests with exaggerated humility and lead them to the best seats.

In the ghetto, there are constant comings and goings. On the one hand, new transports arrive. On the other hand, men are sent – either voluntarily or by force – to work in Poznan. How can anyone keep track of all this?

We also keep moving. By the end of 1941, we have moved from Brzezinska Street to Franciszkanska Street. Here we have a room of our own and we don't have to walk through the rooms of the old couple who are strangers to us. In our room, there is a big bed where my parents sleep and two smaller ones for me and my grandmother. In addition, there is a closet, a table with a few chairs and a big bucket which holds about ten liters. It is used as a chamber pot at night and in the morning it is emptied into the toilet downstairs. On our floor, there is no toilet. It is down in the yard, a simple cesspool, really, with a wooden seat. During the day, we go there to relieve ourselves, as do all the other tenants. There is no tap water in the house; the well is five houses away on the same street.

One day, my father says, "Rysku, please bring two buckets of water. I have already brought two." I take the two empty buckets, pump the well to fill them, and then try to get home with the full buckets. I can barely manage them; I feel so weak. With my last ounce of strength, I drag the two buckets up to the third floor. Out of breath, I tell my father, "I can't do this anymore; I think I have a heart condition."

"You know, Rysku," my father answers sadly, "you are fourteen years old. Mama really can't do it. Look how swollen her ankles are. I have fetched two buckets and you must do the same. We must wash, make soup, clean our room, wash our clothes. It's your duty to help us."

I say, "I can't. I will bring one bucket, but I can't carry two of them!" I am sad that I have failed and burden my parents with this heavy responsibility. But I really am weak and have no strength left.

Soon I am fired from the saddler's workshop due to my lack of skill. Leather is a precious commodity and I am ruining too much of it. They cannot keep me. Actually, I am glad to rid myself of that job – and besides I immediately find a new one.

Tailor's workshop in the Lodz Ghetto.

Messenger Boy in the Tailor's Workshop

Now I work as a messenger boy in the tailor's workshop. It is a good job, because as usual I try to do as little as possible – and I succeed. I have been working there for two years now. Today I go there again; it's always the same route from our house to the workshop in Lagiewnicka Street.

I am accustomed to the sorry sights in the street. People rush by, most of them very skinny with hollow cheeks and pale skin. Those afflicted with tuberculosis are abnormally red. Some people hardly move at all. Their eyes are glassy – they will not survive for more than two weeks. In the ghetto jargon, we call them *Klepsydry*, which in Polish means obituaries.

Well-fed people are rare. Mostly they are the ghetto elite or people working in food distribution, like the men who carry bags of flour, sugar, rye or peas. To lift those 100 kilogram bags, they must be strong and well fed. But how do they manage that, I ask myself, considering the meager rations available?

I have heard that they are thieves. They steal food or "organize" it, as they say. They have a double lining in their clothes. When they carry the bags on the shoulders, they poke a hole in the bag with a pointed object, so that flour or peas leak out. Of course, if they are caught, they could land in prison and that means certain deportation. But they don't care. Hunger and temptation are overpowering.

In this matter, I am a hopeless case. I can't "organize" anything, not even a turnip or a carrot. Therefore, there is no day when I feel full. I am always hungry, hungry, hungry.

But sometimes I am lucky. A young woman lives in our house. She is about eighteen or nineteen, red-haired, freckles on her face, very pretty. I like her from the start and she likes me. "Rysiek," she says, "I am now working in the kitchen for the deportees. Before they go to the train where they get a loaf of bread and some jelly, they receive a thick rye

31

soup and a patty of minced meat in the kitchen from me. The meat patties are counted, so there is nothing I can do. But if you come to the kitchen, I can give you some soup. The train leaves punctually, so you must be there by seven in the evening at the latest. Don't forget to bring a backpack so that you will look like one of the deportees."

Carrying a backpack, I find the food hall. It's full of people, all laden with backpacks, suitcases or bundles. They all talk at the same time. They are excited, filled with thoughts of getting away from the ghetto. Getting work means bread – and bread means life. The mood seems to be positive.

Every day at half past six, I wait in front of the kitchen, greedy for the soup. At seven, "my" girl brings the soup, I wolf it down and run back home. By the time the whistle of the train blows, I am in our room again, happy to be with my parents and my grandmother.

This continues for two weeks, until one day a Jewish policeman stops me on the way home. He asks why I am leaving the railway station. I say, "I forgot my papers and I'm going to get them." He lets me pass. This was the last time I went there. It's true that I miss the lovely soup, but I am too afraid.

Dead bodies lie in front of the houses. Families have no money to bury the corpses, so they wait to be collected. Today there are exceptionally many corpses, and some of them smell of decay. Yesterday was the day when the bread was distributed. Many families hide the dead inside until they get their extra loaves. Thus corpses lie in rooms for up to eight days before they are buried. This is strictly forbidden; deaths are to be reported on the same day. But the hunger is so great that nobody cares. Families risk confiscation of their food ration cards or even prison.

There are also real funerals with family members walking in procession behind the cart pulled by the undertakers, accompanying their dead relatives to the cemetery. The corpses which lie in the streets are picked up by the undertakers, identified, then loaded onto the cart and taken to the cemetery. This isn't such a bad job, since I believe the undertakers get extra soup.

There are others who get extra soup every day. Tied to the carts, eleven and twelve-year-old children pull containers of feces. I don't envy them their nasty work.

The people on the street are all marked by two yellow stars – one on their front side and one on their back. Sometimes one can see a policeman, called an "Ordnungsdienst" in the ghetto, with a cap and an armband displaying the star of David. The firemen and the special

"*Sonderkommando*" unit members wear caps, too. They look healthier; perhaps they also receive extra food rations.

A year and a half ago, an acquaintance of my father arrived from Kielce and immediately became a "big shot" in the *Sonderkommando*. He suggested that my father join this "club." My father refused. "I won't do that!" he said. I am angry at him for this. We would receive more to eat, extra food rations, and be spared from deportation. But he remains stubborn. "I will not become a traitor," he says. I think, instead we will die in this damn ghetto.

But I must admit, I am enduring the ghetto rather well. Instead of working at the *Ressort*. I study diligently. Every day, I take books to work: algebra, history, English, German, physics, chemistry, texts for the second, third and finally the fourth grade of secondary school. I make good progress, and I am sure that I will pass all the tests.

At the workshop, I sit in the waiting room of the manager's office. It is a tiny room without windows, but it has electrical lighting. Here I study and sometimes read a novel I have taken with me for recreation. The only subject I refuse to learn is Hebrew. Firstly I have no Hebrew textbooks and, to be honest, I wasn't anxious to get them. Secondly I would not understand what I am reading, since there are no translations. And thirdly I just don't feel like learning Hebrew.

When the Germans come to check out how the work is progressing, I quickly hide my books. But it wouldn't occur to them that someone would be crazy enough to study in the ghetto.

One of my tasks is to announce the arrival of visitors to the workshop manager. Most of them are tailors, sometimes managers of other workshops, discussing production matters with him. All they talk about is the production. I must also deliver letters, usually ten or fifteen at a time. I deliver them to various places: to other workshops, the accounting office or to the main cash desk. The letters are about production details, additional materials needed, the number of uniforms made, the consumption of raw materials. There are also wage statements, notifications of death and absence – due to illness or deportation. The letters are in a bag I take with me on delivery. There is also a mail book where all the letters are listed, including receipts which must be signed. But, in my opinion, all the paperwork is useless. There are some addressees that are very far away and I don't feel like walking so far. I tear up these letters and fake the signatures in the mail book.

A month ago, I was summoned to the main accountant. He immediately attacked me: Letters, very important letters had not arrived! Did I really deliver them or did I perhaps make a mistake in the addresses?

The thought that I had been destroying valuable mail did not occur to the idiot. Of course, I swore that I had correctly delivered the letters and that the addressees were to blame.

Often I must cross the bridge to the other side of the ghetto to deliver the mail. The wooden bridge connects the two parts of the ghetto so that we won't have contact with the outside world. It's a perfect plan. If we had contact with the Poles, it might be possible to smuggle in food. The bridge is always crowded. From there, I look down on the streetcars, the horse carts and the German policemen guarding the ghetto. These policemen are especially dangerous. They fire at people without warning – sometimes on anything that moves. Either they have orders to terrorize us or they just do it for fun. We are their prey.

It's a good thing that I don't live near the barbed wire fence at the ghetto's border. I would not dare go home after curfew at night. Very often I don't come home until after midnight. Then my parents are paralyzed by fear. They can't sleep. Mama cries and reproaches me for showing no consideration for them. They had already imagined me lying in the streets, shot.

Falling for Fraud

year ago, there was a time when nearly every night I didn't come home until midnight. That was because I came across a gang of hoodlums. They were older boys than I, sixteen or seventeen, and they had an eye on my stamp collection.

Collecting stamps is a hobby of mine. I loved to look at the colorful stamps of the French colonies in Africa, the English King George V stamps, the Belgian ones with a black border commemorating the late Queen Astrid. Several are even of some value; they had cost ten or twenty *groschen* before the war.

I still remember a day before the war when I was sick in bed with bronchitis. My father came home at six as usual. He had a present for me, a stamp that had cost two *zloty*. Two *zloty* was a lot of money, the daily wage of an unskilled worker – a fortune. It was the best present he could have given me. I am deeply moved whenever I think of it. I love him!

It had started in a harmless way with these boys. They too were collecting stamps and I visited them after work to trade stamp. At first, I traded my duplicates. Later, I traded some of my unique specimen. One evening, they ask me: "Do you play poker? Stamps are getting boring. We know your collection already and you know ours. We could play poker for stamps. That would be fun."

I immediately agreed. I had often watched my father and my uncle play bridge and sometimes poker, and I was convinced I could be a good player. The thrill of the game was important to me. It made me forget the hunger which had been tormenting me for years.

I lost the game. And each time I lost more stamps. When I came home, I was so annoyed that I couldn't sleep. Nevertheless, I went there again almost every night. I wanted to win back my stamps. But I lost even more.

My stamp album was almost empty when one evening I realized that I had fallen into the hands of a gang of cheats. I discovered that they had been signalling to each other with their feet. I was furious and desperate, but I didn't want to get into a fight – they were stronger than I.

I stopped going there, but a large part of my beautiful stamp collection was lost for good. It took me months to recover from that loss. Four weeks ago, I parted with the last of my stamps. I sold them at the community purchasing office and received 13 *marks* – ghetto money of course. I gave the money to my parents. And I swore, never, never again would I gamble!

But I don't want to think about this incident any more. I am sitting in my spot in front of the boss's office. Today I want to study the lesson about the Thirty Years War. On with my work.

Sarah

She is younger than I – maybe ten years old, eleven at the most. I meet her while receiving our bread ration from the cooperative. Holding four loaves of bread, she addresses me: "Excuse me, I don't think these loaves weigh two kilograms each. I can not communicate with these people. They don't understand German and I speak neither Yiddish nor Polish. Can you help me? Can you tell them that they must weigh these breads again?"

She has long blonde pigtails and blue eyes; she is skinny and very pale. It is apparent from her face that she has been in the ghetto for a long time. I find her beautiful. In some ways, she is still a child, yet in other ways she is already a young lady. She wears a long cloak, low leather shoes, white knee socks, a white blouse and a pleated skirt.

At first I believe she is the daughter of one of the privileged in the ghetto. It turns out I am wrong: she comes from Germany. She arrived on the autumn 1941 transports of Jews from Germany, Vienna and Prague. Before meeting her, I have never had any contact with these people.

In the tailoring department where I work, there are only Polish Jews. I have heard that those resettled from the *Reich* arrived in regular passenger trains, well-dressed and carrying leather suitcases. They can not understand how they landed in this ghetto. Most of them believe it must be a mistake of some kind. Some of them had fought for their country in the First World War. They were decorated with Iron Crosses and consider themselves German or Austrian patriots, regardless of the Nazis. After a short stay in the ghetto, many die like flies. They are not as strong, as resilient as we are. We have had to survive this dreadful, putrid ghetto for two years now.

I often see Sarah after work and before the curfew. She tells me that in her hometown in Germany she still has many Christian friends. Though it was illegal for Jews and non-Jews to associate with each other,

her friends did not care. Full of pride, she shows me a heart-shaped brooch made of copper, painted red, which she received from one of her girlfriends as a farewell present.

We speak in German, though my command of that language is not very good. My ability to speak German comes from my last two years in school and from what my grandmother who speaks perfect German taught me.

Each time we meet, Sarah looks worse. She has cut off her pigtails and her hair has become shaggy. Her blue eyes, which used to be so lively, stare at me without emotion, as if she can not see me. She has become even more skinny and pale. Each time, she looks more like the sad figures I meet on my way to work, the "living obituaries."

In the ghetto, there are constant deportations. At least 800 people are taken away each day. First there were transports of volunteers. Later when the supply of volunteers dried up, those people with a police record, those on social security and those without a job were put on the lists compiled by Rumkowski. Possibly he also put the names of his adversaries on the lists.

The winter is extremely cold. Temperatures go down to minus 15 degrees Celsius. Those deported are allowed to take 12.5 kilograms of luggage and ten *Reichsmark* with them.

Despite the threat of severe punishments, many whose names are on the list have gone into hiding. If the necessary number of deportees cannot be reached, the Jewish police randomly pick up people from the street and take them to the assembly points.

Due to my working papers, I am spared from deportation, but it still is dangerous to be on the streets. So I see Sarah less and less. I miss her. Although she is younger, I can talk to her about my books. She tells me about her German hometown and her life there before the evacuation. When I am with her, I even forget my hunger.

Like all those do who came here from the *Reich* – from Vienna and Prague – Sarah thinks she is safe from the deportation. She lives with her parents and her grandfather. Her father is an engineer and has found a job in the ghetto. Her grandfather, she tells me, behaves strangely and becomes more peculiar all the time. He rails at the Jews from Eastern Europe, whom he holds responsible for all the misery. He is proud when he hears about the German military victories. He fought in World War I and was decorated with a high medal for bravery.

I can not understand the old man. After eight years of Nazi rule in Germany, after all that has happened to the Jews, he still thinks this way. Isn't this madness?

The German and Austrian Jews who shared the opinions of Sarah's grandfather maintained their loyalty to their home countries to the end of their days. They identified with Germany and considered it a tragic error to be placed on the same level as us, the Polish Jews. They surely loved their native countries – Germany or Austria – hadn't they fought and bled for them in World War One? Like a rejected lover, they were not able to accept the reality: For Germany, they were no longer Germans. Seven years of National-Socialist rule did not change this attitude.

Even today, so many years after these terrible events, many emigrants to Israel and the United States – as well as those who returned to Germany and Austria and are still alive – suffer from this love-hate-complex.

I consider myself lucky because I never experienced this dilemma. I am indifferent to what is called "Heimatliebe" (love of home country). This idea means nothing to me. I don't love them – not the country and not the people living there. But I also do not hate them. Without doubt, I hate the culprits who have not been punished or who have been punished far too mildly. I demand justice. To think that I am utterly powerless in this regard still gives me no peace.

At the beginning of May, those resettled from the *Reich*, from Vienna and Prague, are given their deportation orders. University professors and lecturers, musicians, scientists, retired officers – they came from Berlin, Cologne, Düsseldorf, Hamburg, Frankfurt, Vienna, Prague and Luxemburg. They arrived in the ghetto on regular passengers trains: distinguished citizens, professors, lecturers, musicians, scholars, and former officers. Back then, we observed them as if they were people from another planet. They were full of hope, elegantly dressed, well fed. They did not have the slightest idea of conditions here in the ghetto and what was happening to them. Eight months later, they leave the ghetto, mortally weakened, nearly frozen to death, emaciated and dressed in rags.

Sarah is one of them, along with her parents and her German-obsessed grandfather. I will never see her again.

I hope she did not have to suffer much before dying from asphyxiation.

Food rations become meager.

Hunger

I am hungry.
I am hungry.
I am hungry.

It is the summer of 1942. Finally it has become hot. The deportations are over; the deportees have vanished. I hope they are better off than we are.

The bread ration has been reduced to 250 grams a day. One year ago, we received one loaf of bread, 2 kilograms, for five days – that means 400 grams a day. Soon it became one loaf for six days, then for seven days, now for eight days

Yesterday, my father sent me back to the cooperative: Our bread weighed only 1.9 kilograms. In front of the office stood a long line of people, most of them emaciated with death in their faces. Do I look like that, too? Finally it's my turn. They weigh my bread again and give me the additional 100 grams. It is a good thing that mama divides up the bread every day and hides it from me. Otherwise, I would eat everything at once and starve later.

The bi-monthly food rations are also getting smaller. Currently, we receive 200 grams of flour, 120 grams of brown sugar, 100 grams of rye, 120 grams of margarine, 100 grams of artificial honey, soda, bicarbonate, vinegar, matches, salt, 100 grams of substitute coffee. The coffee isn't too bad when mixed with sugar – at least it fills the stomach. I finish it at once.

But what will tomorrow bring? I hope there is a ration of turnips and potatoes, or else we won't have soup in the evening. Actually, they are no real turnips, but turnips like those we fed to the livestock before the war. I like them. When you are hungry, you will like anything.

At the workshop, the soup constantly gets thinner. There should be 100 grams of potatoes in it, but it depends on how deeply into the pot the serving woman submerges her ladle. She makes sure that her friends and acquaintances get thick soup. But for me, there is often only hot water. Only once in the past few months have I been lucky; for a couple of days, I got thick soup.

Now there are big posters in the ghetto: "Workers wanted for the East! Only one thousand people per day. Twenty-five kilograms of luggage permitted. Transports leave from Radogoszcz Station. Everybody receives two loaves of bread and one kilogram of jam for the journey."

A big temptation! Shall we apply? My parents consider it. Thinking of the bread and the jam, I am all for it. It can't be worse than in the ghetto. My father hesitates; my mother is against it. Grandmother is old and can not work anymore. So the plan is turned down.

We travel through magnificent landscapes in Wales. We visit castles and reside at the best hotels. I am gaining weight again. I cannot restrain myself; I love the English chocolate wafers so much. In Somalia, a million children are starving this year. I read in the Herald Tribune *that it is already too late to help them.*

Dear Hava, my wife, please forgive me. I am probably crazy to think like this. Mostly, the children are affected. And, of course, the old people – but they have at least lived out their lives. The militia soldiers who steal and the relatives of the families who distribute the food do not die from starvation.

I am hungry all the time, all day long. I can't sleep at night; that's how hungry I am. And the damned war just doesn't stop. I am sure the Germans will lose, now that they are fighting the Soviet Union as well as the United States. The only question is: When will it end? I want to be able to fill myself up again, like in the good old time before the war. Rolls or bread with butter, eggs, cocoa – I can hardly remember the taste. I will never forgive mama for putting me on a diet because I was plump. No cocoa, only one egg every two days. And what now? I go crazy with the thought that I could have been eating in advance. Maybe that's not even possible.

After the war, I will sit at a large extended table that fills the whole room. On the table, there will be five loaves of bread and butter and honey and sausages and eggs and jam and sardines. And I will have a big knife in my hand and cut a piece of bread as thick as I desire. And I will spread butter on it and top it with sausages – thick slices of course – and sardines and jam. I will eat until nothing is left and I am full.

But for now, I am left with my empty stomach and the hunger. Each day, I am hungry. Morning and night, I am hungry. And the "eldest" Rumkowski gives us less and less. But for his people, he has special ration cards for the advisory board, the police, the *Sonderkommando*, the firemen, the workshop managers. And we ordinary mortals don't get anything. Too little to live and too much to die.

Sometimes there is only soap available. But I can't eat soap. It's green with the inscription "RIF" and a number. Are the Germans so badly off that they must label their soap?

We must usually sell off our sausages and meats, since we don't have enough money to redeem the standard rations. Sometimes we also need to repair our shoes or to mend our clothes – for which we need to buy sewing needles and fabric. My father says that meat and sausages are not very nutritious anyway. We should look for oil and margarine instead, since they are rich in calories. I don't know if he is right, but we must sell off something, since we don't possess foreign currency or jewelry.

Grandmother has earrings with big diamonds that are worth a lot of money. If we sold them, we could get ten or twenty loaves of bread and I could eat my fill again at last. But she has no mercy and refuses to hand them over. She wants to set up a medical practice for my uncle, the doctor, after the war. Maybe she's right. In a week or in a month when the bread is gone, I'll be hungry again – and my uncle will never get his practice.

I think my grandmother no longer gets food stamps. She was scheduled for deportation and therefore does not officially exist anymore. I think mama shares her meager rations with her, but I'm not sure. Perhaps she should sell her earrings. After all, she still has a diamond ring as well.

I like my uncle very much. He is ten years younger than mama and often plays with me. When he completed his medical studies at the Sorbonne, he dedicated his thesis to his parents and to his sister (my mother), to his brother-in-law (my father) and to me, his nephew. I showed the thesis to my friends at school and bragged about it. Now he is in the Warsaw Ghetto. I hope he is better off than we are.

Before the war, grandfather sent money to Paris to finance his studies. Grandfather died before the war; I think it was cancer of the bladder. Sometimes on the Sabbath, he took me with him to the synagogue where he prayed and proudly introduced me to his friends: "This is my *eynikl*, my grandson." It is a pity that he is dead. But maybe it is better that he doesn't have to starve in this damned ghetto.

My father says the Germans have occupied all of Europe and are winning on all fronts. But I am sure they will lose the war. Napoleon also got as far as Moscow and then had to turn back. Russian winters are tough. I hope the German bastards freeze to death there, that arrogant pack. They shall die – and with them their Jewish lackeys, Rumkowski's followers who fill their stomachs at our cost, who receive extra rations and vacations in Marysin, while I am hungry all the time.

For the last two weeks, signs are posted in the ghetto. Rumkowski reminds us of our duty to salute properly. All German officials in uniform or civilian clothes must be saluted; noncompliance will lead to severe punishment. They can go to hell, Rumkowski with them, that old idiot! I don't see any Germans in the ghetto anyhow and, if I do, I try to avoid them. I hope the time will come soon when I can spit on them.

At the moment, I have other worries than these idiotic saluting duties. If a potato or vegetable allocation doesn't come soon, we won't have anything to eat in the evening. Not even that hot water that is called soup. Mama always cooks a big kettle, but there isn't much in it but water. She says water also satisfies. Maybe, but the result is that I have to get up twice at night to pee and then I feel the hunger. At least when I sleep, I am not hungry.

I am hungry, very hungry. When will I be able to eat my fill again? It's driving me crazy.

Gardening in the Lodz Ghetto.

9

My Summer as a Farmer

For a couple of months now, I have been working as a farmer in my spare time. This must be the silliest idea my father ever had. For a small amount of money, ghetto residents can lease a small piece of land to grow vegetables. Seeds and seed potatoes are available at the local community center.

My father was immediately enthusiastic about the idea. We were given a 100 square meter lot in Marysin. The soil was sandy and I couldn't imagine that anything would grow there. But my father was enthusiastic: "We will grow potatoes, cabbages, carrots and radishes and then harvest them in autumn to improve our meager ghetto rations!"

Every week we went out to the fields and cleared our lot of weeds and roots. My father was delighted. He looked lovingly at each little piece of greenery, as if that future tomato or radish would save us. I was tired though, thank goodness, I had rid myself of the work at the saddlery and wasn't very hard-working as a messenger for the tailor's workshop. I considered the work in the field a silly waste of energy.

After all, I had more important plans. For example, at the moment I had to study algebra and was reading a very interesting book. I hoped the war would soon be over so that we would not have to depend on the few vegetables. Also, my mother in her weakened state wasn't convinced that the drudgery was worthwhile. Only my father showed enthusiasm.

I am hungry all the time, every day, regardless of whether it is spring, summer or fall. I want to eat something right now, today! Only inferior vegetables consistently arrive in the ghetto. In the warm season, they are half rotten; in the winter, they are frozen. They are hardly edible and have no nutritious value. As soon as I have eaten the soup with the rotten vegetables, I am hungry again.

I never vomited in the ghetto – despite all that was disgusting and the bad food – except in 1942 when I became ill with jaundice. By that time, most ghetto residents had jaundice; everyone was yellow and funny looking.

To my great amazement, we harvested fresh radishes from our lot in July and ate them at home. My father was overjoyed: "I told you. If we treat them right, the vegetables will grow."

Now it is late summer, harvest time. Full of hope, we walk out to Marysin to our lot. Now even I believe my father's predictions. We have two empty backpacks with us. By the way, we always have backpacks ready in the closet, just in case we are selected for deportation. It is in these backpacks that we will harvest the fruits of our efforts and take them home.

When we arrive, we are greeted by a scene of devastation. Our lot has been vandalized, as have all the neighbouring ones. All the crops have been stolen! Thieves were in the fields and took away the fruits of our labor! Father turns to stone as mama gently strokes his face and tightly holds his hand.

Only I show anger. What a waste of time and energy! I look at my father angrily: "I knew that this wouldn't lead to anything. I warned you. What nonsense!"

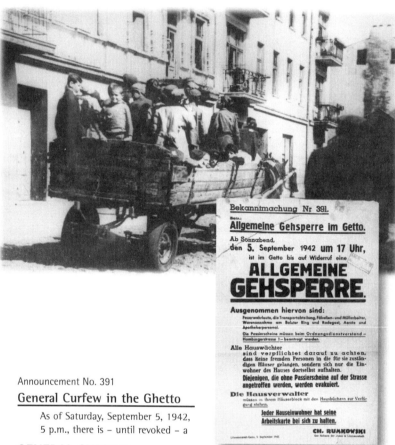

Bekanntmachung Nr 391.

Betr.:
Allgemeine Gehsperre im Getto.

Ab Sonnabend,
den 5. September 1942 um 17 Uhr,
ist im Getto bis auf Widerruf eine

ALLGEMEINE GEHSPERRE.

Ausgenommen hiervon sind:

Feuerwehrleute, die Transportabteilung, Fäkalien- und Müllarbeiter,
Warenannahme am Baluter Ring und Radegast, Aerzte und
Apothekerpersonal.

Die Passierscheine müssen beim Ordnungsdienstvorstand –
Hamburgerstrasse 1 – beantragt werden.

Alle Hauswächter
sind verpflichtet darauf zu achten,
dass keine fremden Personen in die für sie zustän-
digen Häuser gelangen, sondern sich nur die Ein-
wohner des Hauses dortselbst aufhalten.

Diejenigen, die ohne Passierscheine auf der Strasse
angetroffen werden, werden evakuiert.

Die Hausverwalter
müssen in ihrem Häuserblock mit den Hausbüchern zur Verfü-
gung stehen.

Jeder Hauseinwohner hat seine
Arbeitskarte bei sich zu halten.

CH. RUMKOWSKI
Der Aelteste der Juden in Litzmannstadt

Litzmannstadt-Getto, 5. September 1942

Announcement No. 391

General Curfew in the Ghetto

As of Saturday, September 5, 1942,
5 p.m., there is – until revoked – a

GENERAL CURFEW

with the exception of:

firemen, transport department, garbage collection workers,Commodities Receiving
Office at Baluter Ring and Radegast, medical doctors and pharmacists.

Permits must be applied for at the *Ordnungsdienst* Office, 1 Hamburger Street.

All house guards are obliged to ensure that no strangers enter their houses.
Only residents are permitted.
Anyone found on the street without a permit will be evacuated.
Property managers must be available in their houses with a list of residents.

Every resident must be in possession of his employment card.

Ch. Rumkowski
Jewish Eldest of Litzmannsdorf

Litzmannstadt [Lodz] Ghetto, September 5, 1942

10

Curfew and Raid

They are here. "All Jews out!" Shots are heard. We go down to the courtyard and stand in line. Mama pinches her own cheeks and mine so that they are red and we look healthy.

The *Herrenmensch* points his finger: "You, you and you, *you* come with me." Grandmother is one of them. She waves to us for the last time and is taken away in a carriage. An educated woman from a patrician family, she takes her earrings with the big diamonds with her.

We go back upstairs to our room. Grandmother is gone. I hope after the war she can still buy a medical practice for my uncle with the earrings she has taken with her. We could have sold them here in the ghetto, but for no more than ten loaves of bread. Ten breads – that's 20 kilograms! I could have eaten my fill again. Meanwhile, grandmother is gone. I hope she will be able to help my uncle of whom she is very proud.

I sit down at the table, take my Latin book and start to study. "How can you study at a moment like this? I don't understand you," my father says. His voice sounds tired and upset at the same time.

It doesn't bother me. I keep memorizing my Latin words as if the incident didn't concern me, as if I hadn't lost my grandmother ten minutes ago. I don't want to know anything about it. If I shall continue to live, I will need the Latin. In our room, there are now just the three of us, my father, my mother and me.

In all probability, my grandmother was murdered shortly thereafter in the death camp of Chelmo near Lodz. Decades later I followed the media coverage of the legal proceedings concerning that crime. One of the sentences in the Chelmo trial was nine months and three weeks for participation in the murder of 200,000 people. The sentence was passed in the name of the German people.

This equates to less than a second of imprisonment for the murder of an innocent human being, of a baby, of a sick person, of a helpless old man! Not even one second for the murder of my grandmother!

This German court by "right and justice" decided that a Jewish person was not worth more – but at least it recognized that there was wrong-doing in murdering a Jewish person. One second of imprisonment is a punishment after all. So de nominee, the crime was expiated – but still de facto, it has not been atoned.

Two days later they are here again. It seems that the quota has not been reached. This time there are two of them, and they are accompanied by assistants, two Jewish policemen – those miserable creatures.

"All Jews out!" Again we stand in line in the yard. The SS official pulls out a young girl. "You are coming with us!" Her mother wants to go, too. "You stay here." He gives her a kick. In the meantime, the second SS man and the two Jewish policemen search all the flats, they open the closets, look under the beds, search the cellar.

In one of the closets, they find two children hiding, brothers, two boys three and four years of age. They drag them out. One of the boys shouts: "Mama, mama!" The mother steps forward and says a few words to the SS official. He signals with his thumb; she is allowed to accompany her children. The father is allowed to accompany them too. The Jewish policeman drags an old woman out of the house. She was lying in her bed, unable to get up. Like a bundle, she is thrown onto the cart. Then they leave for the next house. The whole procedure doesn't last more than fifteen minutes. We go back to our room.

Ten days ago – but to me it seems like an eternity – Rumkowski called for a gathering. I went there with my father. It was early evening, still daylight. On the square, people gathered, the starved figures of the ghetto. More of them arrived until the square was full. Then he came, our "Kaiser," our king, flanked by men from the Gestapo, the Kripo (criminal police), the ghetto administration and, of course, the ghetto elite.

He stands on the platform and, visibly excited, slowly begins to talk. He speaks in Yiddish. I can't understand the first words; it's too noisy in the square. Then I hear clearly: "The German hyena demands *korbunes* – sacrifices – from us. I have to take your children, and you, all of you know how much I love children. I have to take the old people from you. Put your sacrifices in my hands, so that I can prevent more victims. Otherwise, the same thing will happen that took place in Warsaw."

What does he mean about Warsaw? What does he know that we don't know? "You know how much I love children and what I have done for them!" We don't have a choice. Or else they will come into the ghetto, and then it will be far worse. He keeps talking about "amputation of limbs to save the body," but I stop listening to him.

I don't pity the old man, this traitor, this actor who plays the role of "King of the Jews." His picture hangs in every factory, every workshop, every office. And what now? He can go to hell.

The people on the square start to shout and to cry. They have parents, they have grandparents, they have children. Terror seizes the crowd: "No, we won't hand over our children. We won't give away our parents and grandparents!"

Rumkowski and the other men leave the platform.

The next day, there are posters all over the ghetto: Curfew – no one is allowed to leave the house! Bread for seven days is distributed. Only the very important professions, such as the police or members of the fire brigade, are exempt from deportation.

During the war and during my stay in the ghetto, I despised the Germans, but also their Jewish helpers. After the war, I asked myself how to judge the Jewish collaborators. Today there are attempts to perceive Rumkowski and his assistants as victims themselves, victims who assumed they could save at least part of the Jewish population. Perhaps Rumkowski did not realize at the beginning that this assumption was a mistake. But by March 1942 at the latest, it should have been clear to him what was happening to those who were deported. And with this knowledge, he had no right to decide who would go to certain death – even if in his opinion he could save others. In my opinion, his actions were a crime. It was participation in murder and should be judged accordingly. Only God – if there is such a creator – has the right to decide who should die and when. Had it been otherwise, perhaps I would not have survived. Perhaps the Germans would have destroyed the ghetto earlier and murdered all the residents. But this makes no difference on an historic scale.

The only way to have gained freedom with dignity would have been to put up resistance against the beasts. The absolute duty of the Jewish leader – when he realized what happened to the deported – was to make these facts public in the ghetto and leave all further decisions to each individual to decide his or her own fate. Instead of these three percent of the ghetto population surviving, perhaps an different three percent would have survived. Or maybe no one would have survived. But at least the diabolical plan of the Nazis would have been thwarted. They would have required many more soldiers and the SS to carry out their intentions of the "Endlösung," the Final Solution.

They would have suffered many more casualties due to our resistance, since our people would have defended themselves bravely and furiously if they had known they had nothing to lose. But I believe, in all likelihood, few Jews would have been saved.

The curfew in the ghetto is finally over. The murderous brigade has gone. How many people did they take away in these eight days? How many were shot on the spot? I heard those shots.

We go out on the street again. First for bread – I am hungry. The bread cooperatives are open again. In Brzezinska Street, the old couple who lived in the room next to us has vanished; their flat is empty. My childhood friend Haneczka and her parents are gone, too. Haneczka, with whom I enjoyed playing so much as a child – a black-haired girl with big brown eyes, the companion of my childhood. I will probably never see her again. My teacher, a gifted, educated, honest man, is gone as well. And thousands of others are gone with him. My grandmother is gone, too.

Like a hurricane, those beasts rampaged through the ghetto, rummaging through every house, every corner, every cellar, every closet. Searching for hidden babies, little children, old people or just for people whose faces they didn't like. At will, they shot at the crowds.

How I disdain them, how I hate them, these arrogant scarecrows with their polished boots, with skulls on their caps and those idiotic dictums: "*Unsere Ehre heisst Treue*" (Loyalty is our honour) and "*Gott strafe England!*" (God punish England)

Again I hear Rumkowski the Eldest saying, "Now we are useful to the Germans. We must continue to be hard-working. Now more than ever, because only with our work we will be indispensable to the Germans. Their men are on the front, so they need our work." That fool!

Rumkowski greets Reichsführer Heinrich Himmler,
who expressed his pleasure with the ghetto's production.

'Portrait of Janek, age 15'
Franciszek Jazwiecki

Dreams of Freedom and Comrades

I have eaten magnificently. There were prawns as an appetizer, followed by roast kidney with rice for a main course and green salad, accompanied by a glass of Bordeaux, vintage 1978, and ice cream for dessert. Now I am pleasantly tired. With a full belly, I sit dozing in the armchair of my luxurious villa in the 19th district and listen to music from the radio. As always at this time, the Austrian radio station has classical music. Suddenly I awaken from my doze. My heart starts beating faster. I feel my blood pressure rising. I know that melody. Why does it upset me so much? Where have I heard it before?

It is the autumn of 1942. I have obtained a ticket for the concert at the *Kulturhaus*. There is a symphony orchestra playing Beethoven's *Egmont*. I sit in the concert hall and listen to that wonderful music.

The music lets my hopes flow freely: Freedom is calling. Freedom will be more than just a melody. It will come and I will be free, too – able to move wherever I want, free from war, away from the ghetto. The last notes ring out. Cheers are heard. The audience feels elated, free. Here is one hour in which misery is forgotten.

I am all stirred up. We must fight for our freedom! The melody has given me strength. I must hold my own!

The big deportation is over. I have heard that 70,000 people have been deported. Also those from the *Reich* and from Bohemia are gone. First they were exempted from deportation, but their turn came with the last transports in May. Among them were many non-Jews and baptized Jews, as well. They were transported on different train cars; maybe they didn't want to mix with "ordinary" Jews. According to a German order, each train car was accompanied by a medical doctor and a nurse. This was undoubtedly done to lull the victims into a false sense of security.

And then within 48 hours, all of them were killed in gas cars and buried in mass graves.

I heard about the visit of a high SS officer to the ghetto. He apparently told Rumkowski that the deportees were doing well. Allegedly, they were in a camp in Kolo where ethnic Germans had lived but were now sent east to settle in the Ukraine and Byelorussia. The men were said to be working at road construction; the women were in the camp cooking, washing clothes and taking care of the children.

Nevertheless the people in the ghetto have grown restless. Wagons in big numbers have returned carrying clothing with yellow stars attached. Some of the clothing were bloodstained, and in the pockets identity cards from our ghetto were found.

I eavesdrop and hear a tailor in my *Ressort* say that the Germans are killing the Jews with electric current in rooms especially equipped for that purpose. What nonsense!

The clothes that have arrived are sorted out. The better pieces are intended for the *Winterhilfe*, the winter aid for the poor in the German homeland; the other items remain in the ghetto. I succeed in getting a ration card for a pair of shoes and trousers. The manager of the tailor's workshop where I work as a messenger boy has arranged this for me. The shoes are good. My mother shortens the trousers.

About eight months ago, Julek – a boy in the workshop three or four years older than me – approached me: "Would you like to join our organization?"

"Why? What is your program?"

"We are preparing to fight for a new socialist society. Along with the Red Army led by Comrade Stalin, we will defeat Hitler and capitalism."

"Good," I say, "what do I need to do?"

"First of all, here are two books for you, *The Communist Manifesto* by Karl Marx and *On the Question of Nationalities* by Josef Stalin. Read them and in two weeks time we'll meet again. Then you can tell me if you understand the books and if you have any questions."

I like *The Communist Manifesto* quite well. I agree with the ideas. Stalin's book is boring. I do not understand it and I don't like the name Stalin. I have mixed feelings because I vaguely remember some strange trials in Russia before the war and my father's words: "Stalin is a murderer."

Unfortunately, my father hates the Bolsheviks. He should have tried to escape to Russia with all of us. Then I could have fought against the Nazi rabble and wouldn't have had to suffer in the ghetto.

I now see Julek once a week. He gives me *Das Kapital* by Marx and also books by Bebel and Lenin. I don't understand *Das Kapital*. I have other things to do, like preparing myself for my schooling after the war.

Julek says, "The capitalist conspiracy is responsible for Hitler and the war, but we will overthrow the system. What do you think?" To my timid question asking why Russia made a pact with Hitler, he answers, "That was just tactics." And concerning the trials in the 1930's, he says they were against enemies of the people who had to be destroyed.

Twice he takes me with him to a meeting. Eight boys are there, all of them older than me. They discuss Lenin's theory – two steps forward, one back – and they declare Trotsky to be the worst enemy of the revolution. They never talk about the situation in the ghetto and the hunger. This annoys me, because I am hungry all the time. At the end, we sing the *Internationale* and then we go home.

One day Julek tells me secretively, "Tomorrow you will join me. I want to introduce you to someone." The next day he takes me to a house I have never seen before. In a room, a man sits at the table, partially in darkness. He is a "giant," probably strong as a bear. He points his finger at me and asks Julek, "Who is this?"

"This is Comrade Rysiek."

"How old are you?"

"Fourteen," I reply. The conversation between us is now over. Julek and the giant go on whispering. I can not understand a word and finally we both go home.

The deportations in the ghetto continue. The Jewish police pick up people on the streets to fill the transports. I now see Julek only rarely. Later, I find out he died of tuberculosis, and so I lose my contact to the organization.

One day I meet Ella. I know her from the ghetto school. She invites me to a meeting of the Zionist Youth. I go there. But there are only girls, relatively well dressed and neatly groomed. Apparently they are all daughters of the ghetto elite.

This is even more hopeless than with the communists. At the end we sing *Hatikva* – I prefer the *Internationale*. Palestine is far away; no emissary from there has showed up in the ghetto. And my *tikva* – my hope – is the Red Army, not a country thousands of miles away.

The concert is over. I don't know how I can offer resistance. I have to go back to our hovel. Reality has returned: I am hungry.

Metal working

Apprenticed to the Electrician

For the last four months, I have been working in a metal workshop. I am quite well off; my job is to carry the bag and the ladder for my boss, the electrician. He is not very industrious, which is good for me – I have time to study. Now and then he teaches me some stuff about electricity that I need for my physics lessons. When he changes a fuse, repairs lines or uses machinery, he explains what I need to know for my job.

At work, I get 0.7 liters of soup. It tastes quite good and, if I'm lucky, it contains a couple of potato slices. The woman distributing the soup puts the ladle deeper into the kettle when she knows somebody. I am new to the *Ressort*, so the consistency of my soup is pure chance. With or without soup, I'm hungry all the time. My thoughts revolve mostly around food.

I was dismissed from the tailor's workshop where I had worked for two years. The job was okay; my boss, the workshop manager, was a nice, educated man. The other two messenger boys, Nathan and Szapsiu, always treated me well. They didn't disrupt my studying and minded their own business.

Nathan was a tall, skinny boy, one year older than me. Szapsiu was my age, very short. One day Nathan came to work crying – his father had died from tuberculosis. Shortly thereafter, his mother died. Thus he became an orphan and had to take care of his little sister. Szapsiu only had his mother left and she was sick. I don't know whether he had any siblings. The two messenger boys were at the disposal of the boss. They ran errands for him, fetched his food and coal rations, and did his personal chores.

One day Nathan and Szapsiu are prevented from coming to work and the boss's wife turns to me with a request. She is a nice, attractive woman. She and her husband take care of a little boy whose parents have been deported. They are also friendly toward me.

"Rysiu," says Mrs W, "we received an extra ration of coal, 35 kilograms. Nathan and Szapsiu are not here. Please get the coal and bring it to our home." When I hear the words "extra ration" my pent-up emotions rise. "Get your extra rations yourselves!" I snap at her and sit down to continue studying.

Mrs W rushes into her husband's office and a few minutes later Mr W comes out. "How dare you talk to my wife like that. Get the coal immediately!" In the flush of the moment, I get angry. I tell him to go get his own coal. I am not his servant. In the ghetto, we are all slaves – he, as well. So I lost my job. Thank goodness I found a new one.

Now it is July 1944. Everyone in the ghetto is certain that the Germans have lost the war – my father as well. He is usually well informed, though where he gets his information is a mystery to me. In June, there was a deportation again. They sought people to work in Germany. Some workshops were closed up. Seven thousand people were deported. Many tried to hide. Jewish police selected people from the streets to reach the necessary figures. It is quiet and peaceful now. I hope it will stay quiet like this, so I can finish the course work for the fourth grade of *Gymnasium*.

Some months ago, the Germans needed about 2,000 workers for an ammunitions factory. Lists with names were put together, but people didn't want to go and hid instead. The Jewish police and the *Sonderkommando* rounded up the necessary numbers. First the prisons were emptied. It was dangerous to be on the streets. I am happy that the three of us – father, mother and I – are still together.

The war will be over soon and we will be able to laugh again. We will be happy and not hungry anymore. I remember a Yiddish song that I heard in 1940 from ghetto musicians:

Ikh vel dir dermanen an die troyerike zakhn.
D'vest lakhn, Avrumele, d'vest lakhn.
A zemele mit puter, mit a shtikl hering.
Un dos vet zayn dayn ershter lakh."

I will remind you of sad things,
You'll laugh, Avrumele, you'll laugh.
A roll with butter and a piece of herring.
And this will be your first laugh.

I hope we will be laughing soon. I can already picture us sitting on a richly set table, my parents and I. And there will be rolls, butter and herring.

Everyday there are more transports leaving the ghetto.

Caught in the Mousetrap

August 23, 1944. We are at the railway station. In front of us, a cattle train is ready and waiting. What will happen to us?

Only four weeks ago, I strolled through the ghetto with my friend Mulek. We walked along the wire fence watching the streetcars go by. All the windows were closed. The people inside had their heads bowed and looked away. The weather was nice. At eight in the evening, it was still light.

We talked about our dreams of the Allies' victory and the triumph of socialism – when all people will be equal. No more differences between the poor and the rich, no more oppressors nor oppressed, no exploiters nor exploited. Along the wire fence, we watched a coachman. Apparently, he was drunk and hummed a song, a Polish tango, to himself. The words were: "It is our last Sunday together. Tomorrow we must part forever."

Why did he sing this song? Maybe he knew what was going to happen to us. Was this a warning ? Or was he making fun of us? I don't know.

We are spending our vacation by the lakes of northern England. The hotel is luxurious, an old renovated country house. Our son Michael has gone fishing. He sits by the lake and feels grown-up – I think he is happy. My wife suffers from a painful sciatica inflammation, but she clenches her teeth and doesn't complain. I have a strange sensation of pressure in the chest; I take nitroglycerine pills, but this doesn't help. The sensation is probably not coronary spasms. The weather changes: first the sun is out and then clouds cover the sky. Sometimes a combat aircraft from the British Air Force rushes by above our head. Apart from that, there is only idyllic silence.

After the deportation in June 1944, there is silence in the ghetto – an almost idyllic, misleading silence. The people who were deported are missing forever. I have heard that they were taken to clear the rubble in

69

Germany. The German cities are said to be bomb-wrecked. I also hear that postcards from deportees have arrived in the ghetto saying that they are okay and that they have more to eat than they had in the ghetto.

One day my father comes home very upset. He has listened to the BBC. He whispers to mama that the Nazis have killed 400,000 Hungarian Jews somewhere in Poland.

Why did my father expose himself to this danger? Listening to the BBC is forbidden on penalty of death. People have been shot on the spot for this reason. I am not worried by the stories he tells. Maybe they are just rumors. Besides, I am much more interested in our next food ration. Will there only be turnips again or will there also be potatoes? I am hungry all the time.

Early in August, it is decided that the ghetto with all its residents and machinery will be moved to Germany. Apparently the front is coming closer. Commander Biebow talks to the ghetto residents several times and I listen to his words. "Workers of the ghetto," he begins. Why is he suddenly so polite? I don't like the sound of that! "Litzmannstadt is being bombed and there will be many casualties. It is in your own interest that all the workshops follow orders closely and get ready for deportation. Don't forget to take kitchenware with you, as in Germany there is a shortage. I give you my word of honor as a German officer that nothing will happen to you. Not a hair on your head will be touched."

I don't believe him, nor the word of honor of a German officer. We must hide in the ghetto. Maybe that way we will live to see the liberation.

Each day transports leave. We are still here – but it's getting more difficult. They are making the ghetto smaller and tomorrow the house in which we are living will be outside the ghetto. Suddenly posters appear on all the walls: "Whoever is found in the streets outside the ghetto will be shot according to martial law." Signed by the *Geheime Staatspolizei,* the state secret police.

We must leave our room. But where shall we go? We are trapped. Why haven't we built a shelter? But how would that have been possible? How could we store food when we do not have enough food to eat each day. We have no money, no merchandise – nor do we have a shelter. It is over! We pack everything in our backpacks. Maybe we can hide in a cellar for the interim. Perhaps the deportation will stop and we can stay. There have been several deportations and we are still here. Is this the final liquidation of the entire ghetto?

They keep searching, street after street. Now they are coming! Quickly into a cellar, quickly downstairs! We try to escape, to hide – but the cellar is full. Thirty or forty people are already hiding there.

"Jews, get out!" They have discovered us. They force us into the procession of deportees. Their numbers keep growing. Father says, "Let's try to escape one more time." We run to a door, into the house, up to the second floor. Shots are fired somewhere on the street. I can't see anything. Is someone dead?

For an hour we remain hidden, trembling, without uttering a sound. Silence. It gets dark. The SS moves off. They are afraid to stay in the ghetto for the night.

In the flat on the first floor, there is chaos. The residents have all been deported. There is nothing to eat; they left nothing. I'm hungry. Father gives me a piece of bread from his backpack. Then we go to sleep.

What will happen tomorrow? What shall we do? The most important thing is to stay together.

Early next morning they are back. But they don't rush. I look out the window cautiously. A long procession of ghetto residents, emaciated, marked with the yellow star, are dragging themselves to the railway station. Suddenly one of the uniformed discovers us. "Jews, get out!" Shots are fired. Now they've got us. There is no escape. We must join the procession of people slowly walking in the expanding crowd. Everybody carries a backpack or a bundle – 15 kilograms at the most.

We walk toward an uncertain future – weakened, tired, hungry, without hope.

Flight to save a Torah from destruction by the Germans, Lodz Ghetto.

Arrival at Auschwitz and My First Tallit

Today you say "Shema Yisroel," my son. It is the great day of your Bar Mitzvah, my son Michael, my only child. Yesterday I learned the "Shema" with you. I know you are going to sing your Haftara well. You are a gifted boy and I am very proud of you. I am lucky that you are such a splendid boy. But I would have loved you all the same – even if you were not gifted, even if you didn't come home from school with good grades. Because you are my child, the continuity of my name, the memory of me, the narrator of my stories, the absent witness to the Shoah.

In your Bar Mitzvah speech, you promise to tell my stories to your children. And your children will tell them to their children, so that the story will not be forgotten, can not be denied. So that people will learn that evil is of their own making, that they can easily be infected by evil. So that they will never allow evil inside them to dominate.

The Jewish sacrifice – the sacrifice of the Shoah – must be a warning to every human being. Everyone must draw a lesson from it. Never again must the Jewish people be murdered, robbed and dishonored. Never again must there be a Holocaust of the Jewish people alone. And if it were to be attempted, it should turn into a Holocaust of the entire human civilization.

You stand proud. You put on your new white and black tallit and you say your prayer. The synagogue in Vienna is crowded with people. The rabbi blesses you. I am deeply moved, on the verge of tears. I am happy and thankful that I have lived to see your Bar Mitzvah. And in that moment, I think of another singing of "Shema Yisroel," 48 years ago. Terrible and damned! Is this the price for my survival?

August 24, 1944. Early in the morning, I look through the grated window.

In the train car, stench. The two buckets are full of shit and piss. The children relieve themselves on the spot, crying and screaming. There is almost no air in the car. With fifty people, one can very rarely sit down. The stench of sweating bodies and excrement is hardly bearable. We get one piece of bread for the three of us, my mother, my father and me. I have already eaten my share. We carry our backpacks all the time; each weighs 15 kilograms. There is no room to put them down.

My father and I obtain a seat for mama. Her legs are swollen because of the hunger. She is only 44 years old but looks like an old woman. My poor mama! How lovely her black hair and her nice brown eyes once were. How beautifully she once played the piano and sang me to sleep with her wonderful voice!

The night seems to have no end. Finally, there is daylight; now we are able to see a little. My father stands beside me. The train seems to be slowing down. I read the name of the station: Oswiecim/Auschwitz, written in Polish and German.

Suddenly, my father seems to become older. He looks at us sadly. But we keep moving; the train has not stopped. My father mutters to himself: "I hope we will continue further!" Through the window, I see people in striped clothes marching briskly. They look well fed, not like us half-starved ghetto figures. Was Biebow, the ghetto administrator, telling the truth when he said we would work in Germany and have more to eat than in the ghetto? He also gave us his word of honor as a German officer.

The train stops. The train doors are flung open: "Quick, quick, everybody out!" The luggage remains in the train. "Line up! Men in one row, women and children in the other!" People are confused, desperate. Families are torn apart. The result is chaos.

"Faster, form a line, go!" Whoever doesn't comply is immediately beaten. Shots are fired. I grip my father's hand. We join the line and walk towards a man in uniform. He has a skull on his collar and on his cap.

A man in striped clothes runs by. "How old are you?" he asks in Yiddish.

"Sixteen!"

"Say that you're eighteen," he shouts to me and runs away.

What is going on here? I hold my father's hand tighter and tighter. The main thing is for us not to be separated.

We approach the man in uniform. He sits sedately in a chair and looks bored at the people walking by. With his left thumb, he points in a direction: left or right. In his right hand, he holds a walking stick. He indicates to us to go to the right.

We have not been separated; my father and I stay together. The group of men who stand on the right side are not too old and not too young.

I see a man walking in the wrong direction by mistake. The man in uniform hooks the handle of his walking stick onto his skinny neck and pulls him in the direction meant for him. I stand as though hypnotized. I can not turn my eyes from the handle of the walking stick.

We form lines. "Go on, march, march!" We move on. Mama, where are you? I see in the distance how she slowly walks away from us on her swollen feet, chewing the brown sugar we gave her on her final path. I cannot even say good-bye to her, not even give her a kiss. Does she see me? I don't know.

Walking beside me, a man takes a bundle of dollar bills from his pocket and starts to tear them up. He does this quickly but thoroughly, tearing up the bills in small pieces and dropping them. I am surprised. Where did he get that money? Were there people in the ghetto who actually possessed dollars? I don't want to think about it. I do not care what the stranger does and why.

We are moving towards a shack. Above us sits an SS man in a watchtower. He is very young, probably barely older than I am. He takes a stone and throws it at us. Then he bends down and picks up another one. I become sad. Why does he do that, for what reason?

Today I am not sad. I don't know why. I don't feel compassion, not toward myself, not toward the victims, not toward the offenders. I only feel a choking sensation in my throat. This is the fury I always feel when I think of the past. The rage I feel when I think of the species who call themselves human, even super-human, the species who felt entitled to commit this crime on fellow human beings, a crime unprecedented in the history of humankind! And these crimes are still not atoned for! Earthly justice has failed.

The SS man who threw the stone at us – unless he was killed in the war – has certainly not been called to account. He was only a small part of the machinery and today lives undisturbed somewhere in Germany, respected by his countrymen, loved by his grandchildren, with a clear conscience. After all, he only did his duty. Sometimes, when he reads about the Holocaust or sees pictures of concentration camps on television, I am sure he says, "The Jews should stop with that old business. They just can't keep quiet …"

I sit here at the lake in England and wait – as I have been sitting and waiting elsewhere in Vienna, Paris, Tel Aviv, Cologne or Munich – for a sign of justice, for the nuclear mushroom cloud which will rise over Europe and the whole world and will wipe out all human life on this planet. I am now 64 and am still waiting. I have no hope that this will still happen.

"Spread your *tokhes,* your ass," the prisoner in the admitting zone shouts. "Give us all your hidden money! Your only route out is through the chimneys!"

There is smoke from the chimneys, no birds in the sky, and a stench is in the air. I am standing in the barrack with my father, naked. All heads are being shaved. The barbers work fast.

There is nothing to take from us. These emaciated figures from the ghetto have no money, no hidden diamonds, no gold. After four-and-a-half years, all we have left are rags. And now even those are taken away: we stand naked. An SS man speaks to us in a solemn voice, and a prisoner translates into Yiddish, "Now you will be x-rayed. If something is found, you will be shot immediately. All valuables must be given up now!"

First my father must crawl through a duct filled with stinking disinfectant; then it is my turn. "Dive in fully, you assholes. Faster, faster, go on!" In the next room, we must wait. I'm confused. An SS man with polished boots and a whip grabs some men and drags them out the door. He follows them. Suddenly sirens roar. From the distance, the noise of engines is heard. Lights go out in the room. Is that an air raid warning? Are the British coming to rescue us? I hear saintly voices, people praying: *Shema yisroel adonai elohenu, adonai echad.* I do not pray; I cannot. The lights go on again; the air raid is over. Again an SS man enters, grabs a few men and drags them out.

After the bath, I receive different clothes. They are disgusting rags, smeared with red paint. The jacket and the trousers are much too long for me; the shoes pinch my feet. The socks are made of the fabric of a *tallit*, a prayer shawl. A strange thought occurs to me. In the ghetto, I had no Bar Mitzvah. This is now my Bar Mitzvah. My first *tallit*!

1997. I am standing on that soil again, this time with my son. He asks, "Papa, you were here in Auschwitz. Why don't you have a tattooed number?"

I answer, "They were not sure if they should kill me immediately in the gas chambers or let me die at work. So I was designated a 'depot prisoner' in the gypsy camp of Auschwitz-Birkenau. And for that reason, I don't have a number tattooed on my arm."

They had suffocated the Roma and Sinti earlier in the gas chambers to make room for the new arrivals from Hungary and the Lodz Ghetto. But the name "gypsy camp" remained. And before I received them, a gypsy probably wore the clothes covered with red paint until he was murdered.

'The Jew's Last Road'
Waldemar Nowakowski

Drilled into Concentration Camp Inmates

August 25, 1944. It is night. We march in the direction of the camp. SS men guard our lines on both sides. I stay close to my father. On the left, we pass some barracks separated by an electrified wire fence. Then we walk past an even larger field of barracks, also restricted by wire fence. The gate is opened. We are led into a barrack already filled with people, people wrapped in rags, as we are. We are counted. One better dressed prisoner reports to the SS man: "Space for another sixty!" Where is this space? There is not even enough space to stand!

Will they give us something to eat? Since it's night, I believe they won't.

The sixty people are led in. "Everybody lie down!" the well dressed prisoner shouts. "Lie on your right side. Don't get up and don't turn around!" Threateningly he shows us the stick he is holding in his hand.

"Still up, you pile of shit? Lay down immediately!" He starts beating the man in front of me with the stick. The man screams, cries. We quickly lie down on the ground, one next to the other like sardines, unable to move. There is neither room to lie on one's back nor to turn around.

"Lights out! Quiet in the block!" the prisoner roars. "I am your superior on this block and that is how you must address me. And something else to remember: You are not in a rest home. This is Auschwitz and your only way out is through the chimney!"

The light goes out. Dead silence. People are lying pressed against each other, not moving. They are afraid to move, to speak. I lie next to my father. From the neighbouring block, I hear screams, barking dogs. Something is going on there. Amongst us, tense silence reigns.

An SS man comes by. He looks in briefly and then goes on.

After two or three hours, the block leader suddenly shouts: "Everybody turn around!" We turn with difficulty to the other side, all at the same time.

I am very tired, but I still cannot continue to sleep. I try to think of a history lesson: the French Revolution. Danton, Marat, Robespierre, I repeat in my mind. It doesn't work very well. I won't be able to get books here. And the two I brought along in my backpack are gone. I hope the war will be over soon and I will be able to study again.

At five in the morning, a gong sounds. Somebody shouts," Everybody up!" At last, maybe we'll get something to eat.

"Move! Move!" We step out of the shack. I am cold. Although it is August, it's rather cold outside. My father and I and some other people form a group and try to warm each other with our bodies. It strikes me that we are like sheep in the fields.

The block leader postures in front of us. "Whoever wants to take a crap must report to me and ask for permission like this: 'I am reporting obediently. May I be excused?' Do you understand, you bastards? When the siren sounds, line up in rows of ten in front of the block. Do you understand? The latrine is over there," and he points at a shack. "You have ten minutes at the most. The latrine *Kapo* is responsible for that!"

My father and I ask to be excused. The latrine is in a shack. It is a long wooden board with many holes over which we sit. At least it is comfortably warm in here. I'd like to stay here for an hour. Suddenly the *Kapo* seizes my neighbor, the third man from the right, by the collar and starts beating him: "You are here for the second time, you asshole. I recognize you!" He continues beating him. The man wails, protesting his innocence, which makes the *Kapo* even angrier. I am afraid and run out, even though my ten minutes are not over. Has he killed the man? Probably.

The siren roars. As ordered, we line up in rows of ten in front of the block. The block leader counts us. Then he counts us again. In the meantime, the bodies of those who died during the night have been placed on the ground, also in rows of ten.

The block leader counts us again, this time including the corpses. Apparently there is something wrong, because he races back into the barrack. He is very agitated. A couple of minutes later, he drags out two men, punches them, and with a kick shoves them into the row. Then he begins counting again. It seems that now the number is correct, so he calms down.

Now we have been standing at the square in front of the block for more than one hour. Suddenly the block leader shouts, "Caps off!" Two SS men and a prisoner approach. The block leader steps forward and reports: "Nine hundred prisoners lined up, 48 of them dead!" The SS men inspect and count the prisoners and the dead bodies. Then they leave.

"Caps on!"

We must remain standing. One hour later, the siren roars again. "Move!" the block leader shouts. Roll call is over; we are allowed to move again. "Funeral corps ready!" On the double, several prisoners with stretchers arrive. They load the corpses lying in front of the block onto the stretchers and leave with them.

Now will we get to eat? From the distance, I see some prisoners approach carrying kettles. "Line up!" My father receives a tin bowl and someone with a ladle fills a black fluid into it. It is supposed to be coffee. It tastes terrible! And we must share the contents with another prisoner. Each of us drinks one sip. Biebow had told us that there was a shortage of dishes in the *Reich*. But there are enough bowls here. This is just another means of humiliating us and branding us as animals.

As soon as we have finished drinking, it begins again. "Attention! Line up in rows of ten!" I stand up. "Attention! ... Stand still! ... Move! ... Attention! ... Move! ... Attention! ... Move! ... Caps on! ... Caps down! ... Look left! ... Caps down!" We are being drilled to become "real" concentration camp inmates.

"Now leap-frog! I will show you your place!" I leap like a frog from our block to the next and back. Again and again. I still have not eaten. I am so hungry, so tired. The block leader tries to finish us off. He wears a red band on his clothes, meaning that he is a political prisoner. He is a Pole. And his name is the same as mine: Rysiek.

I don't care anymore – I stop leaping. Angrily he runs over to me and hisses: "What's the matter with you, you lazy scumbag? You are lucky. In 1942, you would have gone through the chimney at once!" he shouts at me in Polish. But now it is the summer of 1944. I look him straight in the face. Astonished, he looks at me, turns around and leaves me alone.

At last we get something to eat. Soup is distributed. It tastes wonderful with big potato slices swimming on the top. Besides, it is thickened with starch flour, much better than in the ghetto. Alas, each of us has to share a soup bowl with a second prisoner. "Stand in line!" We get another soup. The food really is better than in the ghetto; there is only a shortage of dishes.

The sun is warming up. My father has vanished somewhere. I walk along the street. I keep my eyes open, trying not to attract the attention of an SS man or a *Kapo*. The camp is hopelessly overcrowded. The languages one hears are mainly Yiddish, but also Hungarian and Polish. Most people are dressed as I am, in rags that are smeared with red paint. Some are wearing striped prison clothes.

I am tired and slowly walk back to the block. But they won't let me in. They are cleaning it at the moment. So I sit down in front of the block. Finally I see my father coming. "Where have you been?" He doesn't answer. I don't ask again.

"How much bread will we get today? Do you think we'll get another soup in the evening?" He doesn't answer, completely lost in thought.

Through a megaphone an announcement is heard: "The camp commander announces: Whoever finds a louse on himself or on a comrade will receive a loaf of bread as a reward!" The announcement is repeated three times. I have no louse. What a pity. A loaf of bread – I could eat my fill. What does he need a louse for anyway? Perhaps we would all have been killed if lice had been found. They are very much afraid of epidemics, such as typhus.

Finally bread is distributed. A big slice of bread. More than in the ghetto. Accompanying it is that dark fluid they call coffee. I don't drink it. It tastes terrible and this time the tin bowl is dirty and smells.

There is a strange smell in the air. One hears no birds. That smoke is constantly in the air. What kind of smoke is it? Do they cook so much food for the people in the camp? It is said that they burn the dead. Certainly many have died. Last night, in our block alone, there were 48.

At that time, I was only 200 meters away from the gas chambers and crematoria – and still I was unaware of what went on there. I believe this was a kind of subconscious self-protection on my part.

'Square in Front of the Barracks'
Walter Spitzer

The English Lesson

Late summer 1944, in Birkenau. I am memorizing: "*Ich bin* – I am. *Du bist* – you are. *Er, sie, es ist* – he, she, it is."

"Do you know me?"

I turn around and see a boy of my age. "No."

"My name is Leon and I am here with my brother."

I think "so what" and continue to memorize: "*Januar* – January. *Februar* – February. *März* – March. *August* – August. *September* – September." Is it the end of August now or early September? I have lost track.

"You know, I was with old Rumkowski, the Eldest. He liked me very much. I wrote poems that were read in public."

I don't turn around: "*Rot* – red. *Suppe* – soup. *Kraut* – cabbage. *Kohlrübe* ..." I have forgotten the English word for *Kohlrübe*. Damn, what's the matter with me?

"What did you do in the ghetto? Are you alone here?"

Why can't I remember the word for *Kohlrübe*? I go on: "*Messer* – knife. *Löffel* – spoon. *Gabel* – fork."

"Why don't you talk?"

"Leave me alone!" He leaves – finally.

Strange that he loves Rumkowski, the Germans' marionette, the *Verräter*. Okay, *Verräter* – what's the English word? Traitor. *Mann* – man. *Frau* – woman. *Kind* – child."

"*Mennyi kenyeret*," I hear two Hungarians saying. "How much bread?" *Kenyeret* is the Hungarian word for bread. *Krumpli* means potatoes. When will we get food? I'm sure it will be another four hours, maybe longer. I am hungry, as I have been for the last four years – or is it five? 1940, 1941, 1942, 1943 and now summer 1944. It's been more than four-and-a-half years. Nevertheless, the day will come! The war will be over soon. The Germans have lost.

Then I'll be sitting at a table eating several big bowls of potatoes. I'll eat them slowly and with relish. And when I have emptied the first bowl, mama will bring me another bowl, and then another one, until I am totally full.

Where is my father? The last time he disappeared, he came back depressed and nervous. Why? I didn't ask. But he said to me, "You know, Rysiu, my brother and my nephew Jurek were here." That means my uncle and my cousin.

"How do you know?"

"I met someone from Kielce. Mr Proszowski, the doctor who treated you with cupping glasses when you had a cold."

"Where did you meet him?"

"He works in the clothing section. We must try to get out of here. There are transports of workers to Germany."

I begin to understand. Later I become frightened. Where is my father again? I hope he will return soon! I'm lost without him!

I am sure it will be another four hours until we get food. It's noon now. The sun is high in the sky and I am comfortably warm. But I can't sit down or I will risk getting hit in the head with a club by a *Kapo* walking by. So I move on.

The camp street is crowded with all kinds of people. Some wear striped prisoner clothing. Others, like me, are in old rags with red paint on the back, in the front and on the trousers. They speak in Yiddish, Hungarian and Polish. I don't listen.

An SS man approaches, accompanied by the camp commander. They talk to each other amicably. The SS man has polished boots. The camp commander strolls along in his well-cut striped prisoner suit – he is the elite, just like in the ghetto. Who made that suit for him? What badge does he wear? Black? Red? Green? I can't see it. Better not to look in their direction. Better not to attract attention. The two walk past me. I stand at attention. Attention! Cap down! I have been well trained. They leave.

I move on: "*Ich bin hungrig* – I am hungry. *Ich esse* – I eat. *Du isst* – you eat. *Wir essen* – we eat."

'The Transport'
Pierre Mania

Marching Once Again

September 14, 1944. It is night. We march in a narrow column, our steps echoing in the dark. My father walks beside me. I am happy to be near him.

In the camp, we were outfitted with a new set of clothes. No more old rags. Now we are dressed in striped prisoner clothes: trousers, jacket, cap, shirt, undershirt, underpants, socks, even a striped coat. We are real concentration camp inmates. Though I was given good leather shoes, my father received only wooden ones. Before the clothes were issued, we received a bath and a disinfection. Those who looked sickly were sorted out and sent back.

It's a bright night, lit by the moon, the stars and the floodlights. The watchtowers are occupied, the wire fences electrified. To our right is the women's camp. We march by.

Bodies of women hang on the electrified fence, their faces distorted by the grimace of death. Our marching in step sounds like drums on the cobblestones – nightmarish.

Out of the dark, we hear a woman's voice, piercing, desperate, as though coming from the hereafter. "Have you seen Isaak Gottlieb? Isaak Gottlieb from Lodz?" Silence. No answer. The voice again, now pleading: "Isaak Gottlieb and my son Abraham from Lodz?" Eerie, that frightened voice. We march on silently.

The camp is behind us. I turn around for a brief moment. From the chimneys, smoke rises and spreads over the sky.

Now we have arrived at the train station. There is a long line of freight cars. We are counted: forty prisoners for each train car. I cling desperately to my father, trying hard not to be separated.

We receive bread. Everyone gets a big slice, more than in the ghetto. Not bad. I am terribly hungry and begin to devour the bread at once.

Two buckets are put into the car. The door is slammed shut. One whistle and the train starts to move, first slowly, then faster. I hold my father's hand. We are going to an unknown destination.

'The Distribution of Soup'
Max Lingner

The Milk Soup

September 15, 1944. We stand on the site of the roll call. The name of the camp is Falkenberg; the landscape is mountainous. The air is fresh, the weather nice. I am comfortably warm. On our way into the camp, we see prisoners at work. They wave at us and shout in Hebrew: "*Po tov.*" It is good here. I can't believe it. Why should it be better here than anywhere else? But maybe they are right and we will get more to eat in this place. Everything is possible in this up-side-down world.

An SS man looks at us. He is not young anymore – perhaps he is the camp commander. He has a moustache and a beard and he seems almost friendly. He doesn't shout, but asks us quietly, "Why are you so skinny? Where is your homeland?" Next to him sits a younger SS man who plays the harmonica. "I am sure you are hungry," the older one says. "Porter, go to the kitchen quickly. Get some potatoes and tomato sauce at once!"

Am I dreaming? Is this perhaps a trap? "You will receive your kitchenware in the evening. Everyone gets a bowl for the sauce. For now, you can put the potatoes in your caps." The kettles with the hot potatoes are steaming. I get my cap filled with potatoes and a bowl of tomato sauce. As always, I am starved and wolf it down greedily.

"You certainly are hungry. Porter, come here. These people are still hungry. Bring more kettles!" I get another cap full of potatoes and tomato sauce in my bowl. This time a little less. Apparently they have run out of tomato sauce. For the first time in years, I feel comfortably full.

"Now go to the bathrooms and then to the shacks!" The shower rooms are clean and the water is the right temperature, not too hot and not too cold. The wooden shacks are divided in single rooms, all of them with windows. In each room there are six double plank beds. On each of them, there is a straw bag with a cover and two blankets.

I will share a bed with my father. I will sleep on the upper bunk, my father on the bottom one. Time passes quickly; it is already late afternoon. The block starts to fill. People come back from work. One hears Polish, Yiddish and Hungarian. Everyone wears prisoner clothes, but they do not look bad. Apparently, there is more food here.

The block leader approaches my father: "What's your name?"

"Bugajer."

"Bugajer from Kielce?"

"Yes."

"I must talk to you later. After the food ration has been distributed, come to my room."

It begins to rain. At first there are only some drops; then it gets stronger. There is lightning and thunder, a real thunderstorm. I am happy that we are already in the barrack and do not stand outside.

Gong. Roll call. Will we have to go outside after all?

We all stand in the corridor. The block leader counts us. "Seventy-three prisoners reporting. None dead. Attention, caps down!" The camp commander counts again and leaves. "Move!" the block leader shouts and approaches my father. "Now, after roll call, you will get some soup, bread and some extras," he tells him.

The younger SS man with the harmonica is the camp commander. The older one with the moustache, who did the roll call, is the camp leader. An honest man, an Austrian, I am told. They say he was drafted to the SS from the air force. He has forbidden the guards to enter the camp and has given us three days of rest. Strange, I think, Hitler and this camp leader, both are Austrians. What a contrast!

Supper is distributed. There is a rectangular loaf of bread, 1,800 grams among four people. Unbelievable! This is nearly twice as much as we got in the ghetto. In addition, each of us gets a cube of margarine and a spoon of artificial honey. We, the newly arrived, receive dishes and spoons. And than comes the greatest surprise: several kettles of soup!

I can't believe my eyes: milk soup with noodles. I immediately ask my neighbor, a boy from Hungary, "Is it like this every day?"

"No, there is milk soup only once every two weeks. But the other soups are also not bad. Every third day, we get a loaf of bread among three people."

I save half the loaf for the next day. It's a good thing, since we receive only half a liter of substitute coffee in the morning and a thin soup at work for lunch.

"How do you cut the bread?" I ask the Hungarian.

"I ground my spoon on a stone. Then it is easy to cut the bread. I suggest you do the same."

I go to my room and lie down on the bed. Of course, by now I have finished the bread completely. Why should I think of tomorrow? What nonsense!

I wait for my father for a long time. He has gone to see the block leader. He doesn't seem to come back. I'd like to sleep, full and tired as I am.

Finally my father is here. He arrives with the block leader Mr. Picharter and both seem to be pleased. "Rysiek, isn't that your name?" Picharter asks. "Your father will not go to work. He will sweep the rooms and keep the beds orderly. After the food distribution in the evening, you will wait to see if I call you. If there is any soup left, you will get it." With that, he leaves.

"What did you talk to him about?" I ask my father. "I will tell you sometime. Sleep, now." I sleep and dream of a kettle filled with milk soup and noodles, but I can't seem to reach it. Every time I put my spoon in, the kettle vanishes.

The gong sounds. It is early morning. I wake up and look down. My father is there. I am happy, so happy to know that he is with me!

Later I found out what my father had discussed with the block leader. He made a written agreement with that man that half our property would be transferred to him after the war. In return, my father could stay in the block and would not have to go out to work – and in the evenings, we would get leftover soup when it was available.

'Medical Examination'
Auguste Favier

The Interesting Skull of an Ethnic Jew

Octtober 1944. Yesterday there was a roll call for youth. I had been told not to go to work. Young people were ordered to stay in the camp because a medical commission was coming.

I am accustomed to commissions. In the Lodz Ghetto, they came regularly. For example, they inspected the production. They checked whether everything was running well, whether all orders were filled, whether too much fabric was used. It was usually people from the ghetto administration or from the *Wehrmacht* who came to inspect the ghetto. I had never personally experienced a medical commission in the ghetto. I heard that in 1941 or 1942 ghetto residents had been examined and stamped, but I was not there. And during the curfew in the ghetto, there was no commission. It was a deportation and the Germans just rounded up the people. I wonder who will come today.

At noon, there is a roll call. A high ranking SS official shows up, apparently a medical doctor. We are grouped by birth years: 1926, 1927, 1928, 1929, 1930, 1931, 1932. There are no younger children in the camp.

The SS man orders those in the age groups between 1929 to 1932 to step aside. Now it is my turn, birth year 1928. The SS man studies us. Then he walks directly toward me and inspects my head. He circles round me and carefully studies my head.

Then he calls me and another boy out of line and says, pointing at me: "This is a typical ethnic Jew. Those two stay here." The others, born in the year 1928, must join the younger age groups. The SS man doesn't look at the those born in the years 1926 and 1927. He just tells the camp commander who is also present, "They stay here. The others will go to a youth camp." He departs and we are allowed to leave as well. I am very proud that he called me *Rassejude*, an ethnic Jew.

Now I stand naked in front of an SS doctor. The examination is very thorough. Lung and heart are auscultated with a stethoscope. Then the doctor examines us for inguinal hernia, a rupture of the groin. He takes notes diligently and records the numbers of the comrades destined for the youth camp. I am allowed to stay and am happy not to be separated from my father, even though they say work is easier in the youth camp. I don't work too hard anyway. And the main thing is: I stay with my father.

It is seven o'clock in the morning. I stand in front of the mirror and shave. At nine, I must be in my clinic to examine the patients. I inspect my face, the shape of my head, my nose, my ears, my forehead and do not see any special racial characteristics. What did the SS doctor mean back then when he called me a Rassejude? *What did he plan to do with my skull? Was he planning to give it to Professor Hirt as a birthday present for his anatomical skull collection in Strasbourg?*

This "great scholar" Professor Hirt worked for the SS research office "Ahnenerbe" (Ancestor Heritage) and diligently collected evidence for the theory of the "subhuman creature." In June 1945, he escaped justice by committing suicide. On his orders, Hauptsturmführer Dr. Bruno Beger and Dr. Hans Fleischhacker travelled to Auschwitz to select prisoners with special racial characteristics for his collection. They chose 79 Jewish men, two Poles, four men from Central Asia and 30 Jewish women. They transferred them to the Natzweiler concentration camp, murdered them using gas and brought their "fresh" corpses to Professor Hirt in Strasbourg. After a ten-year investigation, a court in Frankfurt held a trial against the two anthropologists Dr. Beger and Dr. Fleischhacker and on the basis of the jury's decision on March 5 and April 6, 1971 pronounced the following judgements:

Dr. Fleischhacker, a lecturer at the Frankfurt University until the beginning of the trial, was acquitted because it couldn't be disproved that he went to Auschwitz solely to test new methods of measurements. Another doctor was acquitted on the grounds that he falsely believed it was permitted to kill Jews who had been selected for death under the supervision of university scientists for a "scientific purpose." Though he helped to murder in large numbers and acted culpably, he had had no evil motives.

Beger, whose name was used for the entire project – "Auftrag Beger" – was given the minimum sentence for aid to murder: three years in prison. Meant for a thirty-year-old, this sentence was given to a sixty-year-old who in addition had waited ten years for his trial – poor man.

I never found out what happened to the other boys, my companions back then. I think they were all sent to the gas chambers. A couple of years ago, I read a report that possibly described their fate.

On October 17, 1962, during a search near the ruins of Crematorium 3 in Birkenau, a half-liter preserving jar with a tin lid was found near the gas chamber. In the bottle was a notebook wrapped in waxed material. The handwriting was that of Salmen Lewental, a member of the Sonderkommando *who tried to record his experiences for posterity. The fragmented notes were written in Yiddish. Under the title "Di 600 yinglekh" (the 600 youths), the following is reported:*

"In bright daylight, 600 Jewish boys between twelve and eighteen years of age were brought to the square. They were dressed in long, very thin striped suits. On their feet, they wore torn shoes or wooden slippers. The boys were good looking and well built, so that not even the rags disfigured them. It was the second half of October. Twenty-five heavily armed SS men led them to the square. When they arrived, the commander ordered them to take off their clothes.

"The boys noticed smoke rising from the chimney and realized at once that they were being led to their death. They started to run around in wild horror and to tear out their hair, not knowing how to escape. Many of them burst into tears. A terrible lament arose. The commander and his assistant began beating the defenseless boys, forcing them to take off their clothes. When his club broke, the commander took another one and continued hitting the boys on their heads until force triumphed.

"Filled with an instinctive fear of death, the boys took off their clothes. Naked and barefoot, they crowded together to protect themselves against the heavy blows. They refused to move. One brave boy walked up to the commander standing nearby and asked him to spare his life. He promised to do the heaviest labour. In response, the commander gave him several blows on the head with a heavy club. Many boys ran up to the Jews of the Sonderkommando, *throwing their arms around their necks and begging for help. Others ran from the large square in an attempt to escape death. The commander called for help from an* Unterscharführer *with a rubber club.*

"The young, clear voices of the boys rose and finally turned into bitter crying. Their terrible lament could be heard from afar. Everybody stood paralyzed by the sound of their pathetic crying. Without a sign of pity, with smirks of satisfaction and victory on their faces, the SS men forced the boys into the bunker, giving them heavy blows. On the steps, stood the Unterscharführer *with his rubber club. Some boys tried to escape. The SS men followed, clubbing them until the situation was under control and all the boys were driven into the bunker. The pleasure of the SS was indescribable. Have they never had children themselves?"*

I read the following entry in the diary of events at Auschwitz-Birkenau for October 20, 1944: "In the gas chamber of crematorium, three, a thousand youths between the ages of 12 and 18 were killed. Among the dead are 357 young Jews who arrived this day from a secondary camp of Grossrosen Concentration Camp."

Falkenberg was a supplementary camp of Grossrosen. In all probability, my friends were in the group mentioned. I was saved by a fluke: the sudden good mood of an SS murderer who found my skull interesting.

'Life in the Camp'
Anonymous

The Reckless Optimist

Winter 1945. It is comfortably warm behind the stove. Outside there is biting frost. It looks like a winter dream, all white around the barracks, and I am sitting in a heated room.

The others must toil outside, soaked in thin prisoner clothes. The foremen from the *Organisation Todt* and the SS men at least have warm coats. They are building fortifications and tunnels. Why are they still building? Why must they work so hard? Why do they fight? They have already lost the war. I could have told them this in 1939. They are out of their minds. I hope they all croak.

Those who are here are actually in not too bad shape. Every day, they bring pieces of coal hidden in their coats so that I can heat the room. It is strictly forbidden to use products essential to the war effort for civilian purposes – and coal is one of them. I am sure they will throw me out. But I hope they won't report me. If they do, I will be hanged for sabotage!

It really was good luck that I was ordered to work here. I was supposed to look for wood and roots in the forest, saw it up, stack it and dry it for the winter, so that during the work breaks they would have a warm room. But I always collected wood for the next three days only. The war will be over soon anyway, so why should I make the extra effort? Now I am in trouble. There is no dry wood in the forest. Everything is wet, damn it. I have won and lost again. I am a damn idiot!

One of the foremen, a civilian with a swastika in his buttonhole, always looks at me angrily. Rightly so, because about one month ago I watched him eating with delight only part of his carefully wrapped buttered bread and hiding the rest in the closet. I waited until he had left, took the bread and cut off a small slice. I liked the taste very much. In the evening, he came into the room, looked at the bread on his shelf, but didn't say anything. The next day, the game continued. This time I cut off a bigger slice. That evening he looked at me angrily but passed me by without saying a word. The next day he hid the bread so well that I couldn't find it. But I am sure he can be dangerous for me!

I'm really crazy. I should have guarded this line of work like the apple of my eye. It was such good luck to get it, or rather chance – like everything else in my life.

That one-eyed SS man, our convoy leader, is a brute. I hope the Russians shoot him in the second eye. We work with a pick and shovel for nine hours. I feel I will be dead soon. The one-eyed bastard plays the same game each time. He turns away pretending not to see us, but he watches us with his one good eye. When one of us stops working, he turns around with lightning speed and strikes him mercilessly. But I am not so stupid as to take a break. I watch him and when he starts his game and pretends not to pay attention to us, I work especially hard. Only when he turns to me, do I put pick and shovel aside. When he stands in front of me, I look him calmly in the eye and report that I need a break. I'm a gambler, putting all my eggs in one basket – he could kill me. He looks at me with his single eye, surprised. But this damn SS man praises me: I am his best worker. Therefore I get an extra soup. As a diligent and honest prisoner, the next day I am sent to take care of the Germans' dwelling.

But now I have lost this wonderful job. My silly optimism – to think that the war would be over soon! But maybe it will be over soon.

The crazy ethnic German in the uniform of the *Organisation Todt* is a strange fellow. He speaks to me in Polish and drags me into a hut to sing the Polish hymn "Poland is not yet lost." A madman? And he never gives me anything to eat.

Really, as far as food is concerned, there is not much here for me. The Germans always get a good soup at lunch time. But afterwards, the kettles are empty. I try to scrape out a little with my spoon, but there is nothing left. The Germans are hungry themselves.

One time I ate my fill. Again it was chance. When the kettles of soup didn't arrive on time, the Germans, excited, angry and hungry, went back to work. In the shack, only two SS men and I remained; both were maybe nineteen or twenty years old. At two o'clock, the soup was finally delivered.

"Open the kettles!" they order. Inside the kettle is a thick pea soup with bits of meat. A wonderful scent spreads throughout the room. The two fill their bowls and tuck in. I wait. "Take as much soup as you want!" What luck! Quickly, I eat one helping, another one, and a third one – before they change their minds. It tastes wonderful. I am close to bursting. "Get your people. We will share the soup." I call everybody who is nearby. As always, the kettles are picked up at three o'clock. In the meantime, so that I won't feel too good, the two of them tell me: "We may have lost the war, but you won't live to see it." Even though they gave me soup, let them go to hell! After work, the other Germans come back to the camp. The two SS men tell them that no soup was delivered. I wish I had another bowl of soup at this moment to forget my troubles and my fears!

The Ukrainians appear in their black uniforms. What are they doing here? They have their own camp in the woods. Maybe I can hide with them. The Germans avoid and disdain them. One time I went to their place. "Why don't you fight with the Red Army against the Germans?" I asked. They chased me away. They speak no German, only Russian. But they are no POWs and they wear those beautiful black uniforms. Uninteresting.

Maybe the Germans won't report me. Maybe that damned war will be over soon!

I constantly need to scratch my belly. It's that strange bandage we are ordered to wear. They check to make sure we wear it and are quite strict about it. A bandage around the belly? Is it supposed to keep us warm? What is the reason for it? And that injection into the chest muscle? Did the SS doctor want to vaccinate us? Are they carrying out experiments? Who the hell knows!

Even today I don't know what kind of medical experiments the Germans conducted on us.

Somebody enters the barrack. I jump up and grab the broom – one never knows who is coming. But it's only the captain of the *Schutzpolizei*. He takes off that funny cap and puts it on the table. He always talks aloud to himself and never addresses me directly. I think he wants to tell me something.

He starts talking loudly: "What happened to my family? For months, I have not heard from my wife and my daughters. Königsberg has been bombed!" He sits down at the table, spreads out the newspaper he brought with him and starts reading. I keep sweeping the room diligently. Then he exits, leaving the newspaper behind on the table. Is he leaving me the newspaper as he has done several times before? Probably. Shall I take it to the camp? The camp commander will give me soup for it, I'm sure. It's dangerous, but I have done it several times. A soup is a soup. After all, one must take risks in one's life.

But this time I'm afraid. I will not take the newspaper with me. The firewood problem is making me sick. It's a miracle that they have not done anything bad to me yet and that they keep bringing back coals for heat. I bend over the newspaper on the table and start to read. Nothing is mentioned about big victories – only about miracle weapons. Again, I think the war will soon be over.

"What are you doing here, you damn dirty Jew? Who gave you this newspaper? What are you reading there?" A beast in uniform with a swastika armlet stands before me. I am paralyzed with fear. He will shoot me! "Reporting obediently, Herr *Obersturmbannführer*. I can not read!" He kicks me with his boots and I am out of the barrack. Now it is finally over. No more good job and warm room. It is not the fault of the firewood. Only my carelessness has caused this. Tomorrow I will have to work outside and freeze again.

Why did I call him *Obersturmbannführer*? It just occurred to me out of nowhere. But at least he didn't shot me. I must be crazy – a reckless optimist!

'Work Column'
Ernst Eisenmayer

The Death March

March 3, 1945, Mauthausen. The corpses of our dead comrades are unloaded. The train stands still. It is snowing. We are soaked, trembling with cold, thirsty and hungry – they give us neither water nor food. To quench the thirst we eat snow. It doesn't help.

Why did I persuade my father to leave? He wanted to stay in the Falkenberg camp. He said to me, "Rysiu, I have a purulent wound on my foot; I can't walk. Whatever will happen to me will happen. You must leave. You will survive."

But I didn't let up: "Please come with me. I will help you walk. I don't want to leave you here alone."

Now I look at him. He will not hold out and I am to blame. I dragged him along against his will. I didn't want to leave him behind; they would have shot him. No, the truth is I didn't want to leave him behind, because I was afraid to be without him. I am selfish.

In February 1945, the Falkenberg concentration camp was evacuated. We started marching and reached the next camp, Wolfsberg, within a day. Like Falkenberg, it is a secondary camp of Grossrosen.

The conditions in Wolfsberg camp were not as "harmless" as in Falkenberg. The prisoners slept in straw without blankets; there were not even plank beds. There I met some friends from my school, the Yitzhak Katznelson school: namely Julek Gans and Salek Krakowski. We stay in Wolfsberg for about one week and then start marching westward.

In lines of five or three, we drag ourselves along, escorted on both sides by SS men. The streets leading westward are crowded with refugees *en masse*, all fleeing the Russians. Old men, women and children are walking, some of them accompanied by horse carts or wagons filled with their belongings. Only a few have cars and they must force their way through the crowds.

Every so often on the roadside, I see hanged German soldiers in uniform. They probably tried to desert. Around their necks are signs reading: "I am a coward." On the walls, there is graffiti: "Quiet, the enemy is listening," "final victory," and other such nonsense. From the distance, I can hear the thunder of cannons from the approaching front. It is music to my ears.

The ground is frozen, the route icy and slippery. On the way, an SS man laughingly hangs himself on my arm, so that he won't slip.

Goldberg, a prisoner my father's age, runs about nervously. Since they sent his son away to the youth camp, he has stopped speaking, become mute. He tries to communicate in sign language.

They give us neither water nor food.

Shots are heard. The SS shoot people from our convoy who break down or try to sit.

I support my father as we walk.

We arrive at a village where only three barns are left standing. They push us into the barns. We are not allowed to leave the barns; we must spend the night here. The SS surrounds us with machine guns. Will they shoot us? Within our barn, the air is dense. We stand crowded together, no room to sit. We are thirsty. During the night, many people die. The dead bodies are placed in front of the barn's entrance.

The next morning, we must maneuver over a pile of corpses. Finally there is some air. We receive a few sips of water, but no food. The second night we spend in the barns again. The air is not much better, but since many have died there is more space.

Early the next day, the order is given to march on. We are loaded onto open wagons. We get water and a slice of bread. The train starts to move. It continues to snow. We are drenched, tired, hungry and thirsty. In the open wagons, a brutal fight breaks out. Everyone wants to lean against the more protected sides of the wagon. I fight to help my father sit at the wall, but he is constantly pushed to the middle again. It is hopeless.

A prisoner sits down next to my father. He is from Carpathian Russia. They talk quietly with each other. From what I hear from their conversation, the man tells my father miraculous stories about famous rabbis and Hasidim. My father listens attentively, sometimes asking questions. This surprises me. He has never been religious; he has always been an agnostic. Is he now returning to the religiosity of his ancestors?

In the midst of their discussion, my father turns to me and says, "Rysiu, we will not see mama again. We will not go back to Poland. We will go to Palestine."

The train slows down and finally stops. The village we are entering is Stará Paka; we are in Czechoslovakia. The Czechs notice us; they break through the SS cordon. They bring water to the train. The SS try to chase them away, but they keep returning.

We continue to travel. On the way, Czech workers throw us their lunch bags again and again. I am not able to catch one of them, but it gives me hope. We have not been altogether deserted.

'Morning Sacrifice'
Edmund Georgen

The Death of My Father

March 3, 1945. "Everybody out! Faster!" the SS men on the platform shout. It is afternoon and we arrive at Ebensee, after having been cooped up in the cattle cars. The dead were unloaded earlier in Mauthausen. I am with my father.

Those able to walk must march; those unable are loaded onto trucks and brought to camp. My father can not walk anymore. All at once, we lose sight of each other.

Everything happens so quickly. I am exhausted, thirsty, tired, hungry. I can not think at all anymore. I'm a weak-willed victim in the claws of beasts. I only hear the words "faster! faster!" and see people falling to the ground under the blows of wooden clubs. We form a line and walk uphill to the camp. At the railway station, some of us try to get some water from a faucet, but the guards chase everyone away.

On our way up to the camp, the people along the road shut their windows and close their curtains. They do not want to see us; we are not a pleasant sight. Perhaps we make them remember all the crimes that have been committed. Perhaps they are already fearful of future consequences, since it is obvious that the war is lost. Perhaps they are afraid of the SS or they may simply be indifferent. Or maybe they feel compassion – but without the courage to undertake anything. Whatever their emotions are, they look away and we feel ourselves in a hostile environment, completely at the mercy of the brutal SS and their helpers.

Arriving at the camp, at the square in front of the crematorium, I see my father again. He sits on the ground and looks at me sadly. "Why did you leave me alone?" he asks. "I have been beaten."

Snow is falling; the earth is frozen. For days, we haven't had a single drop of water. We eat snow, which does not quench the thirst. My father is very weak; he cannot stand up any longer. *Lagerkommandant* Anton Gans, the commander of the camp, has ordered that the weak, those unable to walk, should wait at the square in front of the crematorium.

The distance to the ovens will thus be shorter. The stronger ones go first to be deloused and then to the showers.

I stay with my father. The snow continues to fall; it just will not stop. The landscape is completely white, covered with thick snowflakes. It could make a pretty sight, but I just don't have the eyes for it.

My father says to me, "Rysiu, I would like to smoke a cigarette. Try to get me one."

I run over to a medical doctor with whom I am acquainted. "Doctor," I implore, "save my father's life, please! Give him some medicine for his heart! Please, do something for him!"

He answers sadly, "I can not help your father anymore."

Desperate, I return to my most beloved father, with whom I had not been while he was being beaten, whom I didn't defend, whom I can not help anymore. I kiss him. "Help me get up," he says, "I want to see the world one more time."

I support him with my hands and hold him in my arms. "The world is beautiful, Rysiu. I have to die now, but the war will soon be over and you will survive. The Nazis have lost the war. You should...me...."

This, his last sentence, I erased from my memory. It was eradicated, as if I had never heard it, as if it were never uttered. I repressed it completely, even distorted it. I could not live with my father's last sentence, because I was not capable of fulfilling it.

Only 35 years later did I remember his last sentence. It was shocking for me, because it was the legacy of millions of innocent victims, the same sentence scratched by the doomed onto the walls of the anterooms of the gas chambers in Auschwitz, Chelmno, Treblinka, Belzec, Sobibor, Majdanek: "You shall avenge us."

From time to time, a feeling of revenge arises within me, which I believe to be a natural response, nothing extraordinary. I wish for the murderers' death, because only their death would settle the score, at least partially, and would bring with it the possibility of normal cohabitation with the Germans and Austrians.

But on whom should I take revenge? The murderers were to me faceless individuals with skull insignia on their uniforms. I would definitely not be able to identify them. I would not even know how to execute a person; in my entire life I have never held a weapon in my hand nor have I ever hurt anyone. Thus my feelings of revenge live only as wishes in the realm of fantasy and will remain hidden there.

Sometimes I ask myself whether I would even be capable of killing someone who took part in the genocide, should I ever have the power and the opportunity. Would I be able to take the law into my own hands? I hope that I would be capable of doing so – but I am not sure. Now it is too late for such actions anyway. Most of the murderers are no longer alive. And if they are still alive, I wish them mental and physical pain for the rest of their lives. A bullet would only be a favor.

My father lies down on the ground and suddenly falls into a coma. He simply loses consciousness. It is already dark. I lie next to him and try to warm him with my body. I kiss his face. I stroke his white hair. In his last hours, I want to be very close to him. His throat rattles. The throes of his death last two hours, perhaps even longer.

I am tired, sleepy, but stay awake. I want to stay with him until his last gasp. When I sense that he is no longer breathing and his heart is not beating, I pick him up carefully and carry him into the crematorium. There I address one of the inmates who burns the dead: "It is my father. I want to be with him until the flames consume him."

The prisoner, a Pole, snarls at me: "Staying in the crematorium is forbidden." But he lets me stay. Without a word, he takes the body of my father and lays him in the oven. I remain standing there for another few minutes, say a silent prayer in my heart and then go back out to the square. Here I lie on the ice-cold ground and fall asleep.

When I feel that someone is trying to remove my shoes, I suddenly wake up. It is dawn. An inmate, thinking I am dead, wants to take away my shoes. When he realizes I am still alive, he stops immediately and continues walking in search of other dead bodies. There are no living comrades left on the square.

I am the last one to go to the showers and then to the block.

Dictated to my son Michael on March 3, 1995.

'Corpses in Front of the Railroad Station'
Aldo Carpi

Ebensee

I t is already evening when I get to the block. Darkness lies in the barrack; it is half empty. The kettles with soup are full, a sign that few prisoners are left on the block. Most of them have probably died on the square in front of the crematorium. Now I could eat as much soup as I like. But it is of no interest to me. The severe loss, the death of my father, has robbed me of my will to live. He was my best friend and my support.

I drink a little water and lie down on the space assigned to me on the plank bed. I am tired. I am empty. Nothing matters to me.

The SS men rage like madmen in the barracks. They have dogs with them. It doesn't impress me anymore. I feel no fear. The SS men have brutal faces which convey nothing good. Maybe it is better that my father is dead. Here it is hell. Finally I fall asleep.

In the morning at five o'clock: roll call. The SS men and their dogs appear. We are counted. After the roll call, a Polish prisoner named Jozek asks me, "Where do you come from? Are you alone here?" He is a young fellow, eighteen or nineteen years old. He was deported after the Warsaw Uprising of 1944.

"I am alone. My father died yesterday on the square in front of the crematorium."

"From now on, you will be my assistant, so you will not have to go to work to the quarry. Sweep the room now." I do what he tells me.

The days pass. Room cleaning. Soup. Roll call. Bread. Sleep. Jozek's behavior toward me is decent. Sometimes he gives me extra soup. He keeps me working in the barrack and spares me from the hard labor in the tunnels.

In the meantime, the block has filled with prisoners. They have come to us from other barracks.

After morning roll call, the order sounds: "Report to your squad, line up. Commandos Rella, Hoffmann *und* Maculan, Waagner-Biró, march

115

off!" The comrades march to labor in the quarry. I stay in the block and help Jozek with the cleaning. A young man named Adek helps too.

Constantly I think of my parents. What was the purpose of all the years of pain, all the hunger?

The time of protection in Ebensee soon comes to an abrupt end. After two weeks, it is over, this "pleasant" life. The SS decides that all the blocks with Jewish prisoners must be led by a Jewish block leader. Jozek must go. Before he leaves, he asks his successor to keep me on the block as an assistant.

The new block leader, a Hungarian Jew, who had a special function in the Wolfsberg concentration camp, doesn't like me. I expect nothing good. He has his assistants, his own protégés.

Two days later when the kettles with soup are brought in the evening, the block leader orders me to watch the kettles so that nothing is stolen. Then he goes away. Shortly after he returns, he shouts at me, "You have opened the kettle. You have stolen soup!"

"It is not true, I swear to it." But that doesn't help me. He hits me. I run away and lie down on my plankbed.

Soon after I was fired, the block leader, the skunk, hits Adek on his head. The poor boy goes out of his mind. I am told that he ran half-naked through the camp until one of the guards shot him.

The next day at roll call, I line up. "Report to your squad, line up! To a labor commando! March in lines of five, through the camp gate. Eyes to the left, caps down." We pass through the gate and salute the guard. The path to the quarry is secured by barbed wire. The SS march with us – outside the fence. They always keep their guns cocked. The steps leading to the quarry are uneven. Many comrades tumble down and are dragged along by the comrades who follow. Some are trampled under their feet; they are the first casualties.

I am weak and tired, marching as though in a trance, half asleep with closed eyes. The work in the quarry is hard. I can barely hold the big stone hammer and the shovel in my hands. How can I manage to work with it?

On some days, like today, I succeed in hiding in one of the tunnels. This is fine. Nobody looks for me. I am an unknown newcomer, a nobody, human waste with a number. At noon roll call, I quickly join one of the commandos. The "total number" of prisoners must be correct.

'Workers'
Anonymous

In the Tunnel

I crouch on the ground. I have hidden myself in one of the tunnels. It is cold in here. The walls are wet. Water drips everywhere from the walls.

But anything is better than dragging stones or planks. I can not endure the hard work; this will be my end. I am exhausted, powerless, not able to move from the spot.

They will not search for me, this is for sure. I am no skilled worker and there is considerable chaos all around. But if by coincidence an SS man, a foreman, a Kapo comes by, it could be my end.

Every day I change command, so that they won't list my data and recognize me. But when soup is distributed at lunchtime, the count must be right. This is essential for life. I must take care, regardless of which command I join. Whether it is Rella or Hoffmann *und* Maculan or Waagner-Biró or another one, I must supervene. Anyhow the chaos dominates; only the total number of prisoners must always be correct.

It doesn't matter anymore. I don't believe that I will live to see liberation.

Two days ago, we stood for two hours at the roll call square in the quarry. The number of prisoners was not correct. Finally, after two hours, it became "all clear." An SS man and a Kapo drag two prisoners out of the tunnel. They probably fell asleep in there. The two prisoners are covered with blood – mute, surely already dead. The SS man and the Kapo continue hitting the two of them and only after they have satisfied their desire for murder do they throw them like carcasses onto the pile of dead bodies for today. Now the number is correct. We line up and go back to the camp. "Move!" I walk to my block.

Every day it is the same: caps up, caps down, eyes to the left, eyes to the right. People drop like flies – from exhaustion and hunger.

Not always do I succeed in hiding myself, as I did today. I will not manage this hard labor for much longer, I feel it. Dragging railway ties, even when there are eight or ten of us, is beyond my strength. Dragging, all day long. Some prisoners dodge the work. Too weak to do their share, they do not grasp the load properly. So the whole weight rests on my comrades and me.

One week ago a foremen came to me and asked: "Why are you actually in this concentration camp? You are still so young."

"I am Jewish."

He turned around without a word and walked away. I am foolish; I should have lied! Perhaps he would have given me an apple or a slice of bread.

Three days ago, I had some bad luck. I was standing in line to get the lunchtime soup. An SS man and a civilian with an SS badge in his buttonhole approached. "All the Jews shall report to us. We have easy work for them. They are weak – *muselmann*."

I reported to them. We had to senselessly drag rocks uphill and downhill until dusk. The two officers had a great time. I wish the plague on them. But I don't think I will live to see them hang.

I must be cautious by marching off from the quarry to the camp, so I don't get ordered to carry a corpse. It has already happened to me several times. Although two of us carry the body, it is not heavy: 40 kilograms at the most, usually even less. Even when it was still alive, it was a skeleton. But it is a long way to the camp. It seems endlessly long to me. Carrying the corpse over the steps takes the last ounce of my strength.

After work and when the gong sounds, it means lights out. I walk along the camp street. There is a lively exchange going on. Before my time, bread and food were probably swapped for cigarettes and clothes. Now the "merchants," mostly Russian prisoners, are selling charred bone remains. I suppose they are human bones from the crematorium. A white, clay-like substance is also merchandise for bartering. People buy it to chew on their way to work in order to satisfy their hunger. The Russians try to exchange their goods for cigarettes. Since I do not possess cigarettes, I cannot do any trading.

I meet Jozek on the camp street and ask him, "Do you happen to have a piece of bread for me?"

"No. Do you have cigarettes?" I must say no, too. He looks at me with a searching glance. I see in his eyes that I am already doomed. "I am sorry, I can't help you."

I walk on. Jozek's glance follows me. This camp will be my end.

'The Victory of Death'
June 18, 1944, Felix Nussbaum

The Last Days

May 5, 1945. The block leader distributes bread: one loaf for every four people. First I stretch out my hand and he puts bread into my palm. Then I stretch out my dead neighbour's hand. I am anxious. Will he realize my deception? He doesn't notice. Now I stretch out the hand of my other dead neighbour. He still doesn't notice. Thank goodness!

He walks away and continues to distribute bread. Now I have three portions of bread. I hide two of them under my blanket. The others must not see it. First I eat my own. Carefully, I go for the second portion, then the third and eat them both.

In the night, first one of my neighbours leaned against me; two hours later the other one did the same. Now, in the morning, both of them are dead. Three days ago they were still asking me to help them, to be their *Kalfaktor*, which in camp slang means their servant. They need help getting their food and washing. Both of them are very weak and can hardly move. I am still able to walk.

One of them, a Jew from Prague, lost his entire family. He tells me that after the liberation he will take me with him to Prague, care for me and treat me like his own son. He was rich in Prague. The other one is from Salonika. For both of them, it was not destined to see liberation. Beyond their death, they have left me their bread rations.

In the latter half of April, the chaos is already dominating the camp. We are running short of bread. First there is one loaf for every eight people; finally there is one loaf for every twenty-four. It tastes like sawdust; I am sure they have mixed wood shavings into the dough. The soup consists of water and a few spoons of potato skins. If you happen to find three spoons of potato skins in your soup, consider yourself lucky.

The comrades are dying en masse, like flies. Their deaths are imperceptible and inconspicuous. Now there are not only Jewish prisoners in the barracks, but also Russians, Italians, French, Yugoslavians, Poles – all nationalities.

I am no longer taken to work anymore. I stay on the block.

We have a new block leader, a Polish Jew. His name is Niewiem or Niedzwiedz. He was a butcher in Silesia before the war. He lost his entire family and now he is brutalized, vicious and, in my opinion, crazy. In the evenings, he walks around the block and murmurs to himself in Yiddish: "*Mentshn geyen, mentshen kumen.*" (People come, people go.) With a stick, he brutally hits whomever gets in his way – without reason.

In our group, there are only five boys now – me, Leon, the twins Michal and Iziu, and Mietek. It is good luck that Leon is here. In the block, there is already disorder. The day shift comes, the night shift goes. We don't have a regular place to sleep. Leon is efficient. He makes sure that we have a new place to sleep each night. What would we do without him?

One evening, Leon goes looking for a place for us to sleep. Ten minutes later, he comes back, bleeding from the nose and with a black eye. Niewiem caught him with his stick. Nevertheless, we find a place to sleep.

At night, I lie on my upper bunk and look down. In the dark, I see a Russian prisoner who quietly approaches the neighboring bed. He carefully examines the comrade lying on the bottom bunk, shakes him and ascertains that he is dead. Then he quickly uncovers him and tries to tear a piece of meat from the body. He probably wants to eat it. His hunger is enormous!

Niewiem notices the scene as well. He runs over and slays the man on the spot. Now both are dead, one sooner, one later. We must all expect death here.

A group of prisoners goes to clear the debris in Attnang-Puchheim after the bombing of a train. When they return, they tell us that a food depot was bombed. Meat and food cans were strewn all around and they were able to eat their fill. During the next two days, other comrades go to clear debris in Attnang-Puchheim. I don't have enough strength to report for this work, so I stay in the barrack.

Two weeks ago – or was it three weeks already? I lose track – soup with potato skins was distributed. I was hungry and tried to get hold of a second portion. The room leader, Putterschnitt, distributed the soup in the corridor between the two rooms of the barrack. After I finished my soup, I went to the latrine. There was a small hole leading to the first room. I was already so skinny that I could crawl through that hole. I crawled through and got in line again holding my tin bowl. Putterschnitt recognized me and commanded me to wait.

When all the comrades lay in their sleeping berths, he pronounced the

124

sentence: "The thief" – that is me – "will get 25 cane strokes on his naked buttocks!" I had to lie over the bench with two prisoners holding me firmly, while he hit me. He counted the blows: "One, two, three." I clenched my teeth and didn't utter a sound. After the fifteenth blow, he said, "Now that is enough," and let me go. I returned to my sleeping place. Worried, my friends asked, "How are you? Did it hurt much?"

"I will survive this bastard!" I said and fell asleep.

By early May 1945, I am also a *Muselmann,* one of the living dead. Totally limp, I can barely move. I can not hold the stool that empties under me as a black trickle.

On the second day of May, I pull myself together and drag myself to the sick-bay and later to the *Schonungsblock.*

The block is crowded with living corpses. They lie on two-story plank beds, four to each bed – two face up, two face down. Most of them do not move any more. All beds are already occupied. I lie down on the ground amongst the beds, between two 'neighbors.'

As soon as I arrive at the *Schonungsblock,* they take my clothes away. I keep only my shirt. It isn't cold because of the many people on the block.

One day, when I feel a bit stronger, I take off my shirt while washing. Suddenly, it begins to move. Hundreds of lice hiding in the seams move the shirt on the floor. There are lice of all different colours: grey, white, green ones, small, medium, large ones, some with crosses on the back, some without. I try to stamp out the lice and clean the shirt. But this is a hopeless venture. The remaining lice reproduce at such speed that my shirt remains just as bug ridden. Perhaps they have come from the lice-infested shirts of my comrades. And yet my head is without vermin. Even the shaved stripe in the middle of my hair is clean. I have lice in my clothing only, but these remain plentiful.

On the third day of May, the bread rations are increased. Again there is one loaf of bread for every four people. The block leader and the guards suddenly turn polite. They don't hit us anymore. This is a sure sign of the approaching LIBERATION.

Father, mother, take care of me from above! Help me live to see the day of liberation! It is now a matter of days for me, perhaps only hours.

I have survived and Putterschnitt has, too. After liberation, he apologized for the thrashing he gave me. He had to maintain order in the barrack and, after all, he didn't hit me too hard. The best evidence of this: I have stayed alive!

Richard Bugajer (front, left) and comrades after liberation.

Rebirth

May 1945. I am in a hospital in Goisern. Diagnosis: tuberculosis of the lungs. Three weeks have passed since liberation from the concentration camp. I run a high fever every day, in the mornings up to 40 degrees Celsius.

This evening, my temperature doesn't drop. I feel a pleasant exhaustion, am very weak. From the expression on the face of the doctor on duty and from the body language of the nurse, I gather they are expecting me to die. This is in keeping with how I feel. The lamp beside my bed is covered with a cloth so that the light will not disturb me.

I have a feeling of happiness, tranquillity and relaxation; I have no pain. I think about being reunited with my father very soon; I will set my eyes on his beloved face again. I feel within me love for him and the desire to be with him. I fall asleep, happy and peaceful in the expectation of death.

The American soldiers were not prepared for the situation they found in Ebensee and in the other concentration camps. They don't know how to take care of us, nor do they have the necessary supplies. So in the first couple of days after the liberation hundreds of prisoners die – among them many who couldn't be helped, but also those who suddenly received too much to eat and whose bodies couldn't tolerate the sudden increase of food intake.

I am in the *Schonungsblock* and hear that we youths from the camp will be brought to Switzerland to recover. I report to the Americans and, together with others, am taken to Bad Ischl. Big tubs of hot water are placed in the main square of the town and we are washed and scrubbed by the local women. Afterwards, we are brought to the mobile hospital-train stationed in Bad Ischl, where we are handed over to German nurses and doctors, now prisoners of war, who will take care of us.

These people – who two weeks ago probably cheered Hitler and the Nazis and maybe were Nazis themselves – spare no pain to diligently take care of us. For the first time in many months, I am lying in a bed covered by a white sheet! I receive several meals a day, some freshly cooked here, but mostly from American tin cans from the depots nearby.

One day, I got a tablet of Cebion, a form of vitamin C, left from German supplies. Even today I still remember that taste on my tongue; it seemed wonderful to me.

I am still very weak and move only with great effort. My neighbour, a young Ukrainian of my age, is stronger. Every day, he gets up at five in the morning and walks to nearby farms to get additional food. When he returns with the food, he shares his loot with me, even though he doesn't know me well. I don't know whether he begs or steals. Later, I lose track of him.

After ten days in the hospital-train, we are brought to Bad Goisern to what was once a girls' school. There the Americans have set up a hospital for sick concentration camp survivors. It is called "US Army Hospital 904." I feel a bit better. The only thing that worries me is a recurring fever with major fluctuations in body temperature. In the mornings, I always have a fever up to 40 degrees; in the evenings, my temperature drops as low as 35.7 degrees. I am so weak, I am convinced I have a heart disease. After we are examined and I am x-rayed, it turns out that I suffer from an active case of tuberculosis; the sputum findings confirm this.

We do not remain in Goisern for long. Soon we are moved further to *Hotel am See* in Bad Aussee. Beds are prepared for us on the ground floor. Sick prisoners from the German *Wehrmacht* are housed on the floor above. Thus the atmosphere is strained and I am afraid. I don't know why. Probably it is because the Nazi criminals are close at hand and I feel it inside. Other comrades have died of such fears. For me, the fear causes a miracle: My diarrhea suddenly disappears.

In June 1945, the Americans transfer us back to Ebensee, where transports are being organized to return former prisoners to their home countries. But here in Ebensee, we must now sleep on the bare ground. Fearing the spread of epidemics, the Americans have burned the straw bags.

I enter the hospital where a sign at the entrance states: "Attention! Typhoid and tuberculosis!" The American doctors visit us twice a day wearing masks on their faces. They ask every one of us the typical questions: "You *scheisserei? Viel Wasser trinken.*" (Do you have diarrhea? Drink lots of water.) This is the recommended treatment. Of course, food is in abundance.

128

From Ebensee, the first transports of former prisoners leave for their home countries, first the French, the Dutch, the Spaniards and the Italians. Later the Poles, the Czechs and the Russians go home. The sick, including me, are brought back to the hospital in Goisern, where the doctors and nurses of the established hospitals take care of us.

We young people form a group of diverse nationalities and religions, but we are united by our destiny and survival. I have many Jewish friends, but also some gentile Poles and Russians. Five Russians from Azerbaijan try to persuade me to come to Azerbaijan with them, since I am alone, having lost my entire family. There will be enough to eat in Azerbaijan – bread and potatoes. "You will learn something in our home and you will be fine with us," they assure me. But I have other plans. They leave for home shortly thereafter. I hope that they were not immediately locked up again in a Gulag by Stalin.

My waves of fever come to an end one day. The night before – still in hospital in Ebensee – I had sweated through four blankets. There was even a puddle under the bed from sweat droplets leaking through the blankets. It was a horrible night. But in the morning the fever was gone.

So I am "healthy" again in Goisern. I get a pneumothorax treatment for my left lung lobe which must be refilled with air every three or four weeks. Nevertheless I am well and begin to study with great zeal. I desperately want to graduate from high school and then go on to university.

The Jewish relief organization, the "Joint," pays a teacher to visit me, Mr. Kling, who visits me in the hospital. He receives soup and other food here. He puts in every effort to teach me algebra, Latin, German, English and a little natural science. Two years later, I learn that Mr. Kling was the *Kreisgruppenleiter* of the NSDAP, the district group leader of the Nazi party in the area. In 1947, he is arrested in Vienna by the Americans.

The single year I spent in Goisern seems like ten or twenty years to me. It is just like school vacation: When I was seven or eight years old, the two months of summer vacation seemed endless. Perhaps my time in Goisern seemed so long to me, because I experienced a kind of rebirth there in 1945 and therefore had similar sensations as if I were still a child.

This year is one of the happiest in my life. I hardly have any money, but I can't say I have nothing. Every two weeks, the Americans give us parcels which contain cigarettes. Since I don't smoke, I sell the cigarettes and get *Reichsmark* in exchange.

So I feel like a well-off man. I can afford visits to the cinema and sometimes a train trip to Bad Ischl. I also receive clothes from the Americans, donations collected in America for concentration camp survivors. A nurse kindly made a shirt for me from a bed cover, so I wear a blue and white checked shirt.

After five-and-a-half years, the first movie I see in Bad Ischl is a movie featuring Audrey Hepburn. The train from Goisern to Bad Ischl is crowded most of the time, so sometimes I stand on the running board outside the car. There, I feel free and happy.

In Bad Ischl, there is a camp for Jewish DPs, displaced persons, where I have some friends. I also go to Bad Gastein and to Linz, where I visit friends in the DP camps there. Some friends and former comrades have already moved out of the DP camps. They rent private rooms and lead almost normal civilian lives.

Two of those good friends invite me to a party one day. It must have been the end of 1945 or the beginning of 1946. They are not Jews and intend to go back to Poland. They organize a farewell party in their small flat with bacon, schnapps and wine. Two girls are invited as well.

It is a hilarious evening and the two Poles leave for Poland shortly thereafter. Several days after the party, some Americans from the secret service pay me a visit and ask if I was at the party with the Poles. I tell them truthfully, yes. They ask if I noticed anything unusual and whether both men were in the room the entire time. This I really can't remember. Since I was in a festive mood, I hadn't paid much attention. "I don't remember anyone leaving," I tell the Americans. They soon go away.

Richard Bugajer, 1945

130

I later heard that one of my friends had recognized in Bad Ischl the Gestapo man who had sent him to the concentration camp. After secretly observing him for some time, my friend found out that this man always went home from the Café Zauner at six o'clock in the evening. On that special evening of the party, my friend ran the several kilometers to Bad Ischl from his apartment outside the town, accosted his persecutor and shot him. Then he returned to our party.

Epilogue

I followed the Nuremberg Trials in the newspaper. I had hoped justice would triumph. When McCloy pardoned many of the criminals, I began to doubt the victory of justice, yet did nothing. I did not know how to change the course of events. Today I might be more intelligent about it.

In the sixties, I constantly followed the newspaper reports on the German trials. The mild sentences for the murderers, the explanations of the sentences -- all this drove me to despair. It was like a second killing of the victims. They were murdered again.

But I did nothing. I was preoccupied with acquiring an apartment, expanding my clinic, earning money. What should I have done? I did not have contacts in influential legal circles. Israel was under threat and fighting for its existence and the Jews of the world were looking toward the future and not at the past. They were finished with the past. Whenever we discussed this subject, my Jewish friends did not understand me, nor did they agree with me. They finally wanted to have peace. The concern of most of them was: How can I earn money? And when they already had money: How can I earn more money?

Simon Wiesenthal was one of the few who tried to bring the Nazi criminals to justice. He wrote a book entitled *Justice, not Revenge*, but sadly there was neither justice nor revenge. I fell silent and poured over my own thoughts, but spoke about it to no one, because my thoughts were met with disinterest, sometimes even with hostility.

So I resigned myself, realizing I am an absurd Don Quixote for whom there is no demand. Instead I swam with the current, occupying myself with the increase of possessions at which I was quite successful. I was also not aware that the commander at Ebensee, Anton Gans, had been arrested and charged. I discovered only two years ago that, though he had been convicted, he never spent a day in prison. Instead he died a natural death at the age of 77.

The murderers went into hiding, pursued normal civilian professions and were rarely investigated by the courts. Since they were not repeat offenders, there was no danger that they would murder again. The Shoah was, as historian Daniel Goldhagen writes, a perfectly ordinary crime. Yet, if they were ordered to do so and knew they would go unpunished, they might murder and steal again. And if it were the policy of the authority in power, they would murder not only Jews, as

Goldhagen presumes, but also brown-eyed people or diabetics or bald-headed people and they would be infected with hatred toward these people. If they were convinced to believe, for example, that bald-headed people were responsible for the world's misery -- that bald-headed people reproduce too fast and plan to rule the world and kill others -- they would not hesitate to accomplish the treacherous plans developed by the 'genius' of their 'master race.' Their deeds would help them overcome their own feelings of inferiority and frustration and they would consider themselves the saviors of the world.

The trials against the executioners of the Nazi regime also brought something positive, namely precise information about the committed crimes and public awareness of these crimes. No other chapter of human history is as comprehensively documented as the crimes of the Nazis. One reason for this is the thoroughness of the Germans who recorded everything; the other is the existence of the documents from the trials.

Could no other people but the Germans carry out the Holocaust, the mass murder, the genocide of an entire people? No, only the Germans, or more precisely the Germans of that generation, were capable of this atrocity. It was a combination of certain external factors of that time and the character of the German people that made it possible.

External factors had favoured Hitler's seizure of power. Unemployment and the disastrous economic situation; the Versailles Treaty which put too heavy a burden on Germany; the support of the German industry which foresaw large profits from a growing need for armament and falsely believed Hitler could be manipulated, the misjudgement of Hitler on the part of the world's powers and the Vatican who saw him as a bulwark against communism; the weakness of the Soviet Union due to Stalin's murder of millions of the civilian population and the purges in the Communist party and the Red Army -- these were all contributing factors.

Germans of that time lacked an understanding of democracy and, during the war, they developed a blind obedience. Just as they produced the finest precision machines, they used their sense of precision to carry out the Holocaust.

There were other nations in which anti-Semitism was widespread, also capable of murder and robbery. But this would have resulted in more pogroms where maybe hundreds of thousands of Jews would have been killed and their property confiscated. But that characteristic of precision, that perfect planning, would have been missing. This is why the Holocaust is a singular event which occurred only once and hopefully will never be repeated.

Would the Austrians have been capable of carrying out a Holocaust on Jews? In my opinion, no. Even though there is a high percentage of Austrians among the offenders -- a higher percentage than of the Germans -- they lacked two crucial traits: blind obedience and the precision to guarantee the 'success' of the Holocaust. I am glad that today's Germans have a strong democratic conscience, that they have dropped their blind obedience, and that they are not as diligent as they once were.

In German-speaking countries, a phrase has been adopted to describe the terrible death by asphyxiation of millions of people. It is said that people were "gassed" or that they "went into the gas chambers" -- as though they strolled into gas chamber of their own volition. Even the former Austrian Chancellor, Dr. Bruno Kreisky -- whom I regard to be a very clever politician, as well as a renegade and an opportunist -- describes the death of many members of his family this way: 'They went into the gas chambers.' This is either an intentional or an unintentional understatement of the crimes of the Holocaust. It sounds like going for a walk and, instead of walking to the park, they walked into the gas chambers. The only accurate description is as follows: People were lured into a chamber disguised as a shower room and suffocated from toxic Cyclon B.

Language and its use is one of the most dangerous means to manipulate people. With the incorrect use of terms, mistakes and misjudgements arise. I am convinced that many of the jurors who sat in the trials against the Nazi criminals would never have pronounced such mild sentences if the correct words had been used and the crimes committed by the defendants had been described in more exact terms.

For example, the use of the term "war criminal" instead of "Nazi criminal" is absolutely misleading. The people being accused in these trials were not accused of ordinary crimes committed during war. War crimes are committed when fighting in military conflicts, soldiers fighting soldiers on an equal plane. No, in this case the murderers and their assistants purposefully ordered and committed thousands of murders with malice and evil motives. These murders were committed on defenseless infants, children, old and sick women and men, along with robbery and desecration of corpses. These were insidious murders because, until the last minute, the victims were made to believe they were being sent to work in the east or being relocated for their jobs. Cyclon B gas was insidiously produced to be odorless. This word is particularly appropriate: the 'insidious' suffocation of innocent people by gas. Unsuspecting, helpless people were transported thousands of kilometers to be robbed and killed in forests somewhere to the east. This has nothing in common with the atrocities of war and war crimes.

Any indulgence in the punishment of these criminals is not only wrong, but is a crime of its own. Any attempt to diminish the dimensions of the crime or deny it should be condemned by humanity and persecuted. This murder of millions of people was unique in the history of humanity and will remain so.

Language can become a dangerous weapon and can be easily manipulated at any time. A good example of this is that the supporters of the Nazi ideology in Austria apply the term 'national circles' for their twisted ideology. Contrary to the term 'National-Socialist' (Nazi), 'national' is a word which is usually used for people who treat other cultures with esteem and respect, along with their love for and pride in their own country, their people and their culture. One must be cautious not to confuse such patriots with the criminal 'National-Socialists'; they have nothing in common with that Nazi plague.

The main issue with which has occupied me since after the war is the question of guilt. I can only state my personal opinion, whether I am right or wrong. I approach the question of guilt in my own way, even though it causes hostile reactions toward me from both Jewish and non-Jewish circles. I have never believed in collective guilt since this would mean that every individual citizen of a nation is guilty; this does not correspond with the facts. Though I am not religious, I do want to note the story of Sodom and Gomorra: God spoke to Abraham, saying if he could name one righteous man from these two cities, he would spare everyone.

Believing in collective guilt means placing oneself on the same level as the Nazis or the leaders of the Inquisition who blamed all the Jews collectively for the crucifixion of Jesus, the basis for justifying all actions taken against the Jews.

In Germany and Austria during the Second World War, there was resistance against the Nazi regime, even if only by the few. But it is a fact that numerous people were put in concentration camps and executed for their anti-Nazi activities. One must also keep in mind that resistance against the omnipresent Gestapo was nearly impossible during the totalitarian Nazi regime. Whoever ventured resistance was a true hero. A large portion of the population was surely disillusioned with Hitler and did not want to continue the war after the events of 1942.

There is another reason why assigning collective guilt is dangerous. If everyone is guilty, no one is really responsible. This means that the Nazi criminals can repudiate their personal responsibility for these crimes. If one were to draw up a list of the criminals, first the ones who gave the orders would need to be punished; then the ones who carried out those orders; then the informers who betrayed and handed over the Jews; then the blackmailers who robbed the Jews and then handed them over to the Gestapo. Also guilty would be all those who enriched themselves by participating in the robbery of Jewish possessions and finally those who 'aryanized' Jewish property. It should be mentioned that the perpetrators of all the above mentioned groups were mostly Germans and Austrians, but their helpers were from other European countries as well. The guilt of many individuals has never been atoned for. This was the second crime, almost as severe as the first.

Most of the sentences in the Nazi trials were, as already mentioned, very mild. Many ended with acquittals or ridiculously mild sentences. The majority of the perpetrators who participated in the murders have never been called to account for their atrocities, even when there was evidence. Many escaped justice by fleeing abroad with the help of the Vatican and the Red Cross. Justice has not been done and a clear and emphatic condemnation of this mass murder, this singular monstrous crime, was neglected. Thus the moral guilt continuously weighs heavily on the German people, the moral guilt that began when the German people cheered Hitler, then followed his slogans uncritically, adoring their 'Führer' as long as he was victorious in the war.

The moral guilt is not only with the Germans and Austrians. It is also with the neutral Swiss, who left the Jews to their fate and sent them back to death. It is also with the Americans who didn't help the Jews enough, and with the British who refused the Jews entry into Palestine. The war that they fought against Hitler's Germany had nothing to do with their attitude towards Jews. Saving Jewish lives was not terribly relevant for them.

On the evening when I came to the block in Birkenau after disinfection and the lights went out, American aircraft made infrared photographs of the facilities, the gas chambers and the shacks in the camp. But they never tried to bomb the facilities. As far as I know, those photographs never got to the right departments.

It is an unrecognized fact that Hitler and his myrmidons also betrayed the German people. They -- a people who had produced great minds, outstanding artists and scientists, important philosophers and personalities that enriched all of Europe -- were misled and disgraced. After the war, history instruction in Germany and Austria ended with the year 1918. It was difficult to teach the time between 1933 (beginning in 1938 in Austria) to 1945. Too many of the students' parents and grandparents had been involved in the murderous machinery of the Nazis. To expect children to despise their parents and grandparents is indeed an exacting demand. Only now, more than 50 years after the end of that criminal regime -- or maybe in another 20 years when their parents and grandparents are no longer alive -- will the great-grandchildren grow up in an atmosphere that makes possible an objective and honest judgement of the crimes committed in the Shoah. This will also pave the way for an undisturbed relationship toward the Jewish people.

People willingly talk of "forgiving," that the Jews should forgive the German people. I myself will never forgive the murderers of my parents and members of my people or other people. The others, there is nothing for me to forgive, as they have done no harm to me or my loved ones. An individual who 'looked away' during the war out of fear or a person born after the war who can not have been involved in the crimes -- I have nothing to forgive as they have done me no wrong. I cannot speak for those who were murdered. I have no authority to express any view in their name and much less authority to forgive their murderers.

I want to add that I have been living in Austria since 1945. I am not active in politics and so have never been personally attacked. Also my patients, employees and acquaintances have always behaved well toward me. And when I have needed medical help myself, it was given to me lovingly. It also satisfied me that nobody ever said to me, "I like you because you are Jewish." That would have been as awkward as direct anti-Semitism.

Some of my friends feel they are victims or like to play this role. This does not sit well with me. I survived Hitler, I have lived to see his defeat, and so I feel like a victor rather than a victim.

Richard Bugajer receiving his M.D. degree in Vienna, 1953

In 1953, I proudly took my doctor's degree in a borrowed tuxedo – despite being robbed of my school years, despite the concentration camps, despite tuberculosis, despite the loss of my parents and my whole family. Exactly eight years, two months and nine days after liberation, I was the winner. Many Nazis perished and lie in their graves. And the word "Nazi" has become an insult.

My Shadowlife is not based on a diary. Richard Bugajer didn't think of posterity when he was in the ghetto and in the concentration camp; he was too preoccupied with surviving and the hunger and the violence surrounding him.

As fate would have it, Richard Bugajer was unable to finish the record of his memory which he wrote in the last ten years of his life and which he revised again and again. He started with rough reports which he refined into the short stories which have become the chapters of this book.

The chronology here is not consistent. Sometimes a chapter covers several years, sometimes only certain important events. Toward the end of the book – parallel to the tragic drama of the situation – the speed of events increases. Suddenly the cruelties come in rapid succession.

Most of the events Bugajer mentions are documented in historic literature. Thus one can confirm the death march and the arrival at Ebensee which Bugajer's father did not survive in works by Martin Gilbert (1982) and Florian Freud (1989). Some events stay fragmentary and after the long years it is not possible to date them, such as the *Egmont* concerto.

The events in the ghetto and in the concentration camps never left Richard Bugajer. This static past life always hung above his dynamic, successful present like a shadow. There were not only nightmares and memories that returned as a reflex at the sight of potatoes or with certain pieces of music or stage plays. He also suffered from major health problems. For example, tuberculosis prevented his career as a singer for which he longed. An early inflammation of the heart muscles was responsible for many years of pain and fear when he had to live with a pacemaker within his chest.

But Bugajer never laments. No mourning depresses him nor does he spend time regretting the considerable lost fortunes of his family. Instead he looks ahead, foremost for himself as a person, as a victor who doesn't slip into the common role of survivor as victim.

After months of rehabilitation in Upper Austria and Switzerland, he studies medicine and in 1953 proudly takes his doctor's degree in a borrowed tuxedo at the Vienna University. From the poverty of the postwar years, he develops a storybook career – as a doctor as well as a businessman. He buys and modernizes two clinics in Vienna, resulting in personal prosperity, prestige in the Jewish community, and finally the chance to enjoy the pleasant side of life: art, opera, travels, and grand cuisine.

He is well prepared for the career and the cultural appreciation of an educated Viennese citizen. It was not religion, nor the secular variants of Zionism or Communism, that gave him support during the war; it was study.

During the war, he obsessively clings to his studies – when his grandmother is taken away or when he steals moments from his forced labor. He knows how dangerous it is, but he believes the Germans would never imagine that someone would be crazy enough to study in the ghetto. Only the horror of Ebensee – when survival is a question of days, maybe mere hours – is stronger than his thirst for knowledge.

Love is the second strong pillar which supports the boy, mainly his love for his father. Richard walks through the ghetto seeing the dead and the doomed, smelling the spoiled and the decayed, experiencing brutality and murder. All that is bearable as long as he is not separated from his beloved father.

Several times he narrowly escapes the dreaded separation, and when it finally happens and his weak and beaten father dies in his arms, he blames himself. He should not have taken his father on the deadly journey; he should have protected him. He thinks that it is his selfishness that has driven his father to death, and now, for the first time, he is willing to give up. Liberation by the Americans comes just in time.

It is also love that has allowed this book to come into being – his love for his wife, but above all his love for his son Michael-Gury, named after Richard's father not only because of the Jewish tradition. "To you, Michael, I promised to write the story down. I sat at your small bed and you asked me about your grandparents.... You shall know what I experienced in my early youth. You shall read it to yourself and later to your children so that this horror does not fall into oblivion."

But this book has not been written for Michael alone. It offers an opportunity to sons and daughters of other fathers, as well. They will find on these pages in the form of the narrator, Richard Bugajer, two men in different stages of their lives. Two men who talk to them directly and mercilessly.

First there is the boy, a youth like themselves, without mobile phone and Walkman, but blessed with all the frankness and impudence that come with adolescence. Suddenly the spoiled, plump boy is pushed into a brutal unknown world in which he must prove his worth, in which he achieves enormous things, but also sometimes fails.

And then there is the voice of the mature man, the father and grand-father who talks candidly to readers, perhaps like their own father or grandfather has not. This elderly man becomes credible because he neither talks with a raised finger nor in platitudes. He takes a painful journey back into his own life, to the very borders of the bearable. And he does it with great emotions – with love, but also with hate, rage, and the desire for revenge: "From time to time, a feeling of revenge arises within me, which I believe to be a natural response. I pray for the death of the murderers, because only their death would settle the bill and allow us to live together normally with Germans and Austrians. But on whom should I take revenge? For me, the murderers are faceless creatures with skull insignia on their uniforms. I am sure I would not recognize them. In addition, I would not know how to execute someone. In my entire life, I have never held a weapon nor have I harmed anyone. So my desire for revenge will remain a fantasy for the rest of my life."

For decades Richard Bugajer had repressed the last sentence of his father, the sentence that other victims scribbled on the walls of the gas chambers in Auschwitz and Sobibor: You shall avenge us. But when this enormous sentence finally surfaces from his subconscious, he decides on another path, on that of Simon Wiesenthal: Justice, not revenge. Richard Bugajer can not deliberately carry out his father's last wish. But he also waits for justice in vain.

In the newspapers, Richard Bugajer reads again and again that another Nazi trial has ended with a mild sentence. What remains is bitterness: "I sit here at the lake in England and wait – as I have been sitting and waiting elsewhere in Vienna, Paris, Tel Aviv, Cologne or Munich – for a sign of justice, for the nuclear mushroom cloud which will rise over Europe and the whole world and will wipe out all human life on this planet. I am now 64 and am still waiting. I have no hope that this will still happen."

But hope is still a mighty force, hope that the next generations will do better, that there has been a fundamental change on the side of the perpetrators. With a touch of humor he analyzes: "I am glad that today's Germans have a strong democratic conscience, that they have dropped their blind obedience, and that they are not as diligent as they once were."

On the Jewish side, not only the guilt of the collaborators torments him, but also the missing active resistance: "The only way to have gained freedom with dignity would have been to show resistance against the beasts."

His advice to his son Michael aims at strength and at openness: "You should not be afraid; do not feel fear, since the murderers wounded your father but were unsuccessful in breaking him. I remained strong and am proud of it. I hope you too will be strong and that you will always keep in mind that my love for you is big enough to give you strength for your future life – even after I am gone.... Only if you remain strong will you be able to help others, to be supportive and a role model for them. Respect your fellow human beings and never consider love extended to you as weakness, for which it is often mistaken. If you follow these rules, you will be happy in your life. Striving for happiness is placed in everyone's cradle. It is a natural aspiration for all human beings and the path and aim of our existence."

Reinhard Engel
Vienna, February 2000

Glossary and Notes

Introduction:
Mishna: The book is a compilation of Jewish laws, including 'The Ethics of the Fathers'; compilation of ethical maxims and principles from the Bible. Contains scattered oral traditions that were gathered and organized into six books in the second century A.D. The word is associated with the Hebrew root *shana* which means 'to repeat' or 'to learn.'

Prologue:
Shoah: Hebrew for 'devastation, destruction, catastrophe"; used as a common alternative to Holocaust. The systematic extermination of Jews in the Third Reich.

Chapter 1:
Yitzhak Katznelson: A Zionist and poet who wrote mostly in Hebrew. One of Katznelson's three sons, Ben Zion, murdered in 1942 in Treblinka, was a classmate of Richard Bugajer. Katznelson fled to Warsaw from Lodz and was one of the spiritual leaders of the Warsaw Ghetto Uprising. He managed to escape to France with a forged passport and was later interned in a German prison camp in Vittel, where he wrote many books. When the Germans found out that his passport was forged, they sent him to Auschwitz where he and his eldest son Zvi were murdered in April 1944. His Yiddish book *The Song Of The Murdered Jewish People* was written in Vittel.

Tanakh: Old Testament in Hebrew

Techesakna, Hatikva: Hebrew songs. *Techesakna*, which means "become strong," is the song of the Zionist workers movement. *Hatikva*, which means "hope," is the hymn of the Zionist movement and anthem of the State of Israel.

Chapter 2:
Hans Biebow: Businessman and coffee merchant from Bremen who became the Nazi leader of the ghetto administration in Lodz. His initial responsibilities covered the "food and economy administration," and, beginning in October 1940, he was responsible for the entire administration of the ghetto, including 250 German officials. Biebow was not only responsible for the ghetto administration and the production for

the *Wehrmacht* and other customers, but also for the transports of Jews to the concentration camps of Chelmno and later Auschwitz. After the war, he was sentenced to death by a Polish court in Lodz and was executed in 1947. See *Encyclopedia of the Holocaust* (1990).

Chaim Mordecai Rumkowski: Leader of the Jewish Board of Elders, the puppet administration of the Lodz Ghetto, called the "Jewish Eldest." In this position, Rumkowski, who had managed an orphanage in Lodz before the war, was directly under the supervision of Biebow. In daily life, he had far-reaching authority, including a police force of his own, the Jewish *Ordnungsdienst*. Rumkowski also managed the 120 workshops or *Ressorts*. From the end of 1941 on, when the concentration camp of Chelmno was established, Rumkowski organized the deportation of ghetto residents for the Germans. Initially, he did not know they were being sent to extermination camps. Rumkowski and his family were themselves later sent to Auschwitz in the summer of 1944, where they were murdered. See *Encyclopedia of the Holocaust* (1990).

Chelmno: Called *Kulmhof* in German. The first Nazi concentration camp where gas was used for mass murders. Chelmno is 70 kilometers west of Lodz. Mainly Jews from the Lodz Ghetto, Jews from the Warthegau – the western portion of Poland, not part of the *Generalgouvernement*, belonging directly to the *Reich* – and non-Jewish people from other countries were murdered there. Altogether 320,000 people were murdered by the *Sonderkommando Kulmhof*. After the war, a Polish court sentenced two of the commanders to death. Between 1962 and 1965, at a trial in Germany against twelve other Chelmno commanders, three were sentenced to twelve years in prison, one to seven years. The others received mild sentences. See *Encyclopedia of the Holocaust* (1990).

Chapter 4:
Yom Kippur: Hebrew for 'Day of Atonement.' The holiest Jewish holiday, a day of fasting; the last day of repentance beginning with Rosh Hashana.

Chapter 10:
Herrenmensch: German for 'masterful man,' member of the 'master race' (meant ironically here)

Chapter 14:
Tallit: Hebrew for 'prayer shawl.' A rectangular white with black or dark-blue striped cloth made from wool, cotton, or silk, it is worn over

the shoulder by observant Jews during prayers. The *tallit* also serves as a shroud, and, as such, symbolizes mortality.

Shema Yisroel: A Hebrew prayer which begins with the words: "Hear o Israel, the Lord our God, the Lord is one." A prayer of faith, it is part of the daily liturgy and is considered the confessional of martyrs who have used it as their last prayer before death.

Bar Mitzvah: Hebrew for "son of the commandment." At age 13, a Jewish male becomes bar mitzvah, an adult within the Jewish community who is responsible to follow the Jewish commandments. This event is usually celebrated in a synagogue with the young man reading the weekly portion of the Torah and/or the Haftara. Often, he also makes a speech in which he commits himself to observe the rules of the Jewish commandments.

Haftara: Hebrew for 'conclusion.' After the reading from the Torah, there is a part from the Prophets that refers to the weekly portion of the Torah.

Tokhes: Yiddish for 'backside,' 'ass.'

Chapter 16:
Leon: Leon Zelman, who studied in Vienna after the war and has directed the Jewish Welcome Service in Vienna for many years.

Colored triangles: In the concentration camps, colored triangles marked the prisoners according to their 'crime': for example red was for political prisoners, green was for criminals, etc.

Chapter 18:
Falkenberg: Secondary camp of Grossrosen Concentration Camp in Silesia. Wolfsberg belonged to this complex as well.

Chapter 19:
Unterscharführer: A rank in the SS.

Chapter 20:
Organisation Todt: A uniformed working organization named after its founder Fritz Todt. *Organisation Todt* was mainly responsible for the construction of armament facilities on both the eastern and western fronts.

Ukrainians in black uniforms: In all probability, these were members of the Ukrainian SS.

Obersturmbannführer: A rank in the SS.

Chapter 21:
Mauthausen: A concentration camp in Upper Austria. Ebensee was a secondary camp of Mauthausen.

Hasidim: Followers of a traditional religious mystical movement in Eastern Europe.

Chapter 23:
Units Rella, Hofmann *und* **Maculan, Waagner-Biró:** Work units allocated to the construction companies that used forced laborers in the tunnels of Ebensee.

Chapter 24:
Muselmann: A term used in concentration camps for those emaciated, miserable figures at death's door. In this doomed state, they were often dragged to work by their comrades, so they would not be immediately killed.

Chapter 25:
Schonungsblock: German for 'block of protection'; block where the sick, unable to go to work, stayed and waited for their death.

Chapter 27:
McCloy: John McCloy was a US high commissioner in Germany after the Second World War. In 1951, he gave amnesty to several war criminals who had been sentenced in the Nuremberg Trials for less than 15 years; one of them was Alfred Krupp. During McCloy's administration, the Nuremberg Trials were stopped. Later McCloy, as president of the Chase Manhattan Bank, tried with moderate success to get compensation for slave laborers from big companies in Germany. See Friedrich, *Die kalte Amnestie* (1994).

Epilogue:
Aryanizing: This term indicates the transfer without adequate compensation of all property from Jews to persons with 'pure' Aryan (non-Semitic) blood. This transfer was forced on Jews under the Nazi laws.

Dr. Richard Bugajer was born on February 2, 1928, in Kielce, Poland. His father Michael Bugajer came from a family of timber merchants. His mother Luba, born Blawat, was from Lodz, where her ancestors were among the founders of the local cloth industry in the first half of the nineteenth century. Several of Luba's relatives, both on her father's and mother's side (the Dobranicki family), were entrepreneurs who ran cotton spinning and weaving mills and owned property in Lodz.

In the 1930's, the Bugajer family moved from Kielce to Lodz where Richard attended Yitzhak Katznelson's Hebrew school. After the German invasion of Lodz, the school was closed. Richard and his parents were forced to move to the ghetto. For a short time, he went to a school in the ghetto until 1941, when this school was closed as well.

In August 1944, he and his parents were deported to Auschwitz, where his mother was separated and murdered. With his father, he was interned first in Auschwitz, then in several other concentration camps, and finally in February/March 1945 he was transported via Mauthausen to the concentration camp of Ebensee.

On March 3, 1945, his father died in his arms as a result of severe beatings. Though Richard too seemed doomed, he managed to survive and was liberated on May 6, 1945, by American troops. At that time, he weighed 38 kilograms and was ill with tuberculosis.

Of the entire large Bugajer family, only a few relatives who had fled to the Soviet Union survived. One uncle had immigrated to Palestine before the war. All the others were murdered in Auschwitz, Treblinka, and Chelmno.

After liberation, Richard Bugajer was hospitalized in Bad Ischl Military Hospital, then in Goisern. Later he was sent to Davos and Montana in Switzerland for rehabilitation.

Meanwhile he continued his studies and, in spite of his illness, he graduated from high school in 1946. In Vienna, he studied chemistry but had to abandon this field because his damaged lungs could not tolerate the laboratory fumes. He switched to medicine. A talented bass singer, he also studied singing at the music academy.

In 1953, he obtained his medical degree. Although he continued working on his voice, he had to abandon his music studies due to his lung condition and his lack of financial resources.

In the 1950's, he continued his specialized medical training in Paris and London. In the 1960's, he bought the *Helia,* a physical therapy clinic which had been founded in 1900 in Vienna's second district by a Jewish doctor, Dr. Maximillian Neumann. In addition to the *Helia,* he bought another institute for physical therapy, the *Hebe.*

In 1971, Richard Bugajer married Dr. Hava-Eva Bugajer-Gleitman. Their son Michael-Gury was born in Israel in 1979. Richard Bugajer died unexpectedly on June 18, 1998, on a cruise ship near Corfu.

Adelson, Alan (ed.), *The Diary of Dawid Sierakowiak: Five Notebooks from the Lodz Ghetto*, New York, 1996.

Adelson, Alan, and Robert Lapides (eds.), *Lodz Ghetto: Inside a Community Under Seige*, New York, 1989.

Adler, Hans G., Hermann Langbein, and Ella Lingens-Reiner, *Auschwitz, Zeugnis und Berichte*, Vienna, 1994.

Arad, Yitzhak, Yisrael Gutmann, and Abraham Margaliot (eds.), *Documents on the Holocaust*, Jerusalem, 1981.

August, Jochen, *Herrenmensch und Arbeitsvölker. Ausländische Arbeiter und Deutsche, 1939–1945*, Berlin, 1986.

Ausgewählte Probleme aus der Geschichte des KL Auschwitz, Verlag staatliches Auschwitz-Museum, Aktion Sühnezeichen/Friedensdienste, Berlin, 1988.

Barkai, Avraham, *Nazi Economics: Ideology, Theory, and Policy*, New Haven, 1990.

———, *Das Wirtschaftssystem des Nationalsozialismus. Ideologie, Theorie, Politik, 1933–1945*, Frankfurt am Main, 1988.

Czech, Danuta, *Auschwitz Chronicle, 1939–1945*, New York, 1990.

Davidson, Eugene, *The Trial of the Germans, An Account of the Twenty-two Defendants before the International Military Tribunal at Nuremberg*, New York, 1966.

Dobroszycki, Lucjan (ed.), *The Chronicle of the Lodz Ghetto, 1941–1944*, New Haven and London, 1984.

Dobroszycki, Lucjan, and Barbara Kirshenblatt-Gimblett (eds.), *Image Before My Eyes. A Photographic History of Jewish Life in Poland, 1864–1939*, New York, 1977.

Dlugoborski, Waclaw (ed.), *Zweiter Weltkrieg und Sozialer Wandel. Achsenmächte und besetzte Länder*, Göttingen, 1991.

Drobisch K., and D. Eichholtz, *Die Zwangsarbeit ausländischer Arbeitskräfte in Deutschland während des Zweiten Weltkriegs*, in *XIII internationaler Kongre der Historischen Wissenschaften*, Moscow, 1970.

Engel, Reinhard, and Joana Radzyner, *Sklavenarbeit unterm Hakenkreuz. Die verdrängte Geschichte der österreichischen Industrie,* Vienna, 1999.

Encyclopedia Judaica, Jerusalem, 1972.

Freund, Florian, *Concentration Camp Ebensee: Subcamp of Mauthausen,* Vienna, 1990.

———, *Arbeitslager Zement. Das Konzentrationslager Ebensee und die Raketenrüstung,* Vienna, 1989.

———, *Kriegswirtschaft, Zwangsarbeit und Konzentrationslager in Österreich,* in *Österreicher und der Zweite Weltkrieg,* Vienna, 1989.

Freund, Florian, and Bertrand Perz, *Industrialisierung durch Zwangsarbeit,* in Talos, Emmerich, Ernst Hanisch, and Wolfgang Neugebauer, *NS-Herrschaft in Österreich, 1938–1945,* Vienna, 1988.

———, *Fremdarbeiter und KZ-Häftlinge in der "Ostmark,"* in Herbert, Ulrich (ed.), *Europa und der "Reichseinsatz." Ausländische Zivilarbeiter, Kriegsgefangene und KZ-Häftlinge in Deutschland, 1938–1945,* Essen, 1991.

Friedmann, Benedikt, *Ich träumte von Brot und Büchern. Zornige Erinnerungen eines jüdischen Österreichers,* Vienna, 1992.

Friedrich, Jörg, *Die kalte Amnestie,* Munich, 1994.

Fröbe, Rainer, *Der Arbeitseinsatz von KZ-Häftlingen und die Perspektive der Industrie, 1943–1945,* in Herbert, Ulrich (ed.), *Europa und der "Reichseinsatz." Ausländische Zivilarbeiter, Kriegsgefangene und KZ-Häftlinge in Deutschland, 1938–1945,* Essen, 1991.

Galanda, Brigitte, *Die Maßnahmen der Republik Österreich für die Widerstandskämpfer und Opfer des Faschismus — Wiedergutmachung,* in Meissl, Sebastian, Klaus-Dieter Mulley, and Oliver Rathkolb (eds.), *Verdrängte Schuld, verfehlte Sühne. Entnazifizierung in Österreich, 1945–1955,* Vienna, 1986.

Gilbert, Martin, *The Boys. Triumph Over Adversity. The Story of 732 Young Concentration Camp Survivors,* New York, 1997.

———, *The Holocaust. The Jewish Tragedy,* Austin, Tex., 1986.

———, *Atlas of the Holocaust,* New York, 1982.

Goldhagen, Daniel Jonah, *Hitler's Willing Executioners,* New York, 1996.

Grossmann, Mendel, *With a Camera in the Ghetto,* New York, 1977.

Gutman, Israel (ed.), *Encyclopedia of the Holocaust,* 4 vols., New York, 1990.

Hamann, Matthias, *Erwünscht und unerwünscht. Die rassenpsychologische Selektion der Ausländer,* in *Herrenmensch und Arbeitsvölker. Ausländische Arbeiter und Deutsche, 1939–1945,* Berlin, 1986.

Heer, Hannes, and Naumann, Klaus (eds.), *War of Extermination: The German Military in World War II, 1941–1944,* New York, 2000.

Herbert, Ulrich, *Hitler's Foreign Workers: Enforced Foreign Labor in Germany under the Third Reich,* Cambridge, 1997.

——— (ed.), *Europa und der "Reichseinsatz." Ausländische Zivilarbeiter, Kriegsgefangene und KZ-Häftlinge in Deutschland, 1938–1945,* Essen, 1991.

Hilberg, Raul, *Perpetrators, Victims, Bystanders: The Jewish Catastrophe, 1933–1945,* New York, 1992.

———, *The Destruction of the European Jews,* 3 vols., New York, 1985.

Hofer, Walter (ed.), *Der Nationalsozialismus. Dokumente, 1933–1945,* Frankfurt am Main, 1957.

Jacobsen, Hans-Adolf, and Hans Dollinger (eds.), *Der zweite Weltkrieg in Bildern und Dokumenten,* Munich, Vienna, and Basel, 1968.

Jenewein, Jürgen, *Wirtschaftliche Arbeitsleistung von KZ-Häftlingen in Österreich zwischen, 1938–1945,* Linz, 1998.

Judentum in Wien, *Heilige Gemeinde Wien,* Vienna, 1987.

Just-Dahlmann, Barbara, and Helmut Just, *Die Gehilfen. NS-Verbrechen und die Justiz nach 1945,* Frankfurt am Main, 1988.

Kaienburg, Hermann, *KZ-Haft und Wirtschaftsinteresse,* in Kaienburg, Hermann (ed.), *Konzentrationslager und deutsche Wirtschaft, 1939–45,* Opladen, 1996.

——— (ed.), *Konzentrationslager und deutsche Wirtschaft, 1939–45,* Opladen, 1996.

Katzenelson, Yitzhak, *Vittel Diary,* Tel Aviv, 1972.

———, *The Song of the Murdered Jewish People,* Tel Aviv, 1970.

Kendler, Edeltraud, *Nie wieder! Das Konzentrationslager Ebensee, Eine Dokumentation*, Bad Ischl, unpublished monograph.

Klüger, Ruth, *Still Alive: A Holocaust Girlhood Remembered*, New York, 2001.

Knight, Robert, *Ich bin dafür, die Sache in die Länge zu ziehen. Die Wortprotokolle der österreichischen Bundesregierung von 1945 bis 1952 über die Entschädigung der Juden*, Frankfurt am Main, 1988.

Kogon, Eugen, *The Theory and Practice of Hell*, New York, 1950.

Konzentrationslager Ebensee. *Ebensee Concentration Camp*, Ebensee, 1998.

Langbein, Hermann, *Arbeit im KZ-System*, in *Dachauer Hefte. Studien und Dokumente zur Geschichte der nationalsozialistischen Konzerntrationslager*, vol. 2, bk. 2., Dachau, 1986.

Levi, Primo, *The Voice of Memory: Interviews, 1961–1987*, New York, 2001.

————, *The Periodic Table*, New York, 1996.

————, *Conversations with Primo Levi and Ferdinando Camon*, Marlborough, Vt., 1989.

————, *Other People's Trades*, New York, 1986.

————, *The Drowned and the Saved*, New York, 1989.

————, *The Mirror Maker: Stories and Essays*, New York, 1989.

————, *Moments of Reprieve*, New York, 1987.

————, Levi, Primo, *If Not Now, When?* New York, 1986.

————, *Survival in Auschwitz and The Reawakening: Two Memoirs*, New York, 1986.

————, *The Monkey's Wrench*, New York, 1986.

————, *If This is a Man*, New York, 1959.

Lewenthal, Salmen, *Inmitten des grauenvollen Verbrechens. Handschriften von MitglIiedern des Sonderkommandos*, Auschwitz, 1996.

Lifton, Robet Jay, *The Nazi Doctors. Medical Killing and the Psychology of Genocide*, New York, 1986.

Loewy, Hanno, and Andrzej Bodek (eds.), "Les Vrais Riches" — *Notizen am Rand. Ein Tagebuch aus dem Ghetto Lodz, Mai–August 1944*, Leipzig, 1997.

Longerich, Peter (ed.), *Die Ermordung der europäischen Juden. Eine umfassende Dokumentation des Holocaust, 1941–1945*, Munich, 1989.

Luczak, Czeslaw, *Mobilisierung und Ausnutzung der polnischen Arbeitskraft für den Krieg*, Poznan, 1970.

Marsalek, Hans, *Die Geschichte des Konzentrationslagers Mauthausen*, Vienna, 1980.

Meissl, Sebastian, Klaus-Dieter Mulley, and Oliver Rathkolb (eds.), *Verdrängte Schuld, verfehlte Sühne. Entnazifizierung in Österreich, 1945–1955*, Vienna, 1986.

Moser, Jonny, *Die Katastrophe der Juden in Österreich, 1938–1945 — ihre Voraussetzungen und ihre Überwindung*, in Schubert, Kurt, and Jonny Moser, *Der gelbe Stern in Österreich*, Studia Judaica Austriaca V. Eisenstadt, 1977.

———, *Österreichs Juden unter der NS-Herrschaft*, in Talos, Emmerich, Ernst Hanisch, and Wolfgang Neugebauer, *NS-Herrschaft in Österreich, 1938–1945*, Vienna, 1988.

Müller-Hill, Benno, *Murderous Science: Elimination by Selection of Jews, Gypsies, and Others in Germany, 1933–1945*, Plainview, N.Y., 1998.

Neugebauer, Wolfgang, *Das NS-Terrorsystem*, in Talos, Emmerich, Ernst Hanisch, and Wolfgang Neugebauer, *NS-Herrschaft in Österreich, 1938–1945*, Vienna, 1988.

Pingel, Falk, *Die Konzentrationslagerhäftlinge im nationalsozialistischen Arbeitseinsatz*, in Dlugoborski, Waclaw (ed.), *Zweiter Weltkrieg und Sozialer Wandel. Achsenmächte und besetzte Länder*, Göttingen, 1991.

Pus, Wieslaw, *The History of the Jewish Families Dobranicki, Blawat and Bugajer*, unpublished monograph.

Schoeps, Julius H. (ed.), *Neues Lexikon des Judentums*, Gütersloh and Munich, 1992.

Segev, Tom, *The Seventh Million*, New York, 1993.

Semprún, Jorge, *Die große Reise*, Frankfurt, 1981.

Stiefel, Dieter, *Entnazifizierung in Österreich*, Vienna, Munich, and Zurich, 1981.

Talos, Emmerich, Ernst Hanisch, and Wolfgang Neugebauer, *NS-Herrschaft in Österreich, 1938–1945*, Vienna, 1988.

"Unser einziger Weg ist Arbeit," *Das Getto in Lodz, 1940–1944*, Vienna, 1990.

Weinzierl, Erika, *Zuwenig Gerechte. Österreicher und Judenverfolgung*, Graz, 1979.

Wiesel, Elie, *Night*, New York, 1960.

Wiesenthal, Simon, *Denn sie wu ten, was sie tun. Zeichungen und Aufzeichungen aus dem KZ Mauthausen*, Vienna, 1995.

———, *Justice, Not Vengeance*, New York, 1989.

Widerstand und Verfolgung in Oberösterreich, 1934–1945, Vienna and Linz, 1982.

Wistrich, Robert, *Wer war wer im Dritten Reich: Anhänger, Mitläufer, Gegner aus Politik, Wirtschaft, Militär, Kunst und Wissenschaft*, Munich, 1983.

Zandman, Felix, with David Chanoff, *Never the Last Journey*, New York, 1995.

Zelman, Leon, and Armin Thurnher, *After Survival: One Man's Mission in the Cause of Memory*, New York, 1998.

The Publisher gratefully acknowledges the following institutions for the use of works of art in their collections:

Front cover, fragment from an untitled painting of the Lodz Ghetto at night, by M. Schwarz, Jewish Historical Institute, (Zydowski Instytut Historyczny), Warsaw, Poland.

Back cover, Flight to save a Torah, Lodz Ghetto photograph from the Jewish Heritage Lodz Ghetto archive.

p. 60, "Portrait of Janek, age 15," Franciszek Jazwiecki, Auschwitz Museum.

p. 78, "The Jew's Last Road," Waldemar Nowakowski, Janina Jaworska, Warsaw.

p. 84, "Square in Front of the Barracks," Walter Spitzer, Auschwitz Museum.

p. 88,"The Transport", Pierre Mania, Pierre Mania, Rouen, France.

p. 90,"The Distribution of Soup" Max Lingner, Private Collection, Paris, courtesy Rutledge Press, NY, published in Art of the Holocaust.

p. 94, "Medical Examination," Auguste Favier, Robert Favier, Villeurbanne, France.

p. 100, "Life in the Camp," anonymous, The Commission for the Study of Nazi Crimes, Warsaw.

p. 106,"Work Column," Ernst Eisenmayer, Documentation Archive of the Austrian Resistance (Dokumentationsarchiv des österreichischen Widerstrandes), Vienna.

p. 110, "Morning Sacrifice," Edmund Georgen, Museum of the Two World Wars, (Musée des deux Guerres Mondiales), Paris.

p. 114, "Corpses in Front of the Railroad Station," Aldo Carpi, Ghetto Fighters'House (Beit Lohamei Haghetaot), Israel.

p. 118, "Workers," anonymous, Club of the Former Inmates of Ravensbruck, Warsaw.

p. 122, "The Victory of Death," Felix Nussbaum House, Osnabrück, collection of the Savings Bank of Lower Saxony.

The photographs from the Lodz Ghetto used in this volume are from Jewish Heritage's Lodz Ghetto archive.

AGMV Marquis

MEMBER OF SCABRINI MEDIA

Quebec, Canada
2002